AF269135

Where the Wind Blows

Vitality Among Friends

Jay W. Marshall

EARLHAM
SCHOOL *of* RELIGION

Richmond, Indiana

Where the Wind Blows: Vitality Among Friends

Published by Earlham School of Religion Publications, an imprint of Earlham Press, 228 College Avenue, Richmond, IN 47374. All rights reserved. Except for brief quotations in connection with a literary review, or use of material in the appendix, no part of this publication may be reproduced, stored in a retrieval system, or transmitted, in any form, or by any means, electronic, mechanical, photocopy, recorded, or otherwise, without the prior written permission of the Earlham School of Religion.

Cover design: Judi Marshall and Tim Seid

Library of Congress Cataloging-In-Publication Data

Marshall, Jay, 1959-
Where the Wind Blows: Vitality Among Friends/ Jay Marshall
ISBN 978-1-879117-15-0

   1. Religion   2.Quakerism

2005905612

*To the Religious Society of Friends,
in celebration of what we have been,
what we are,
and what we yet shall be.*

Table of Contents

Prologue

In 1998, Earlham School of Religion conducted a national consultation during which Friends discussed their hopes and fears regarding the state of the Religious Society of Friends. The published results of the consultation, *Among Friends,* contain much worry and fear, centered largely on the issues of declining membership and money. Interspersed among these anxious comments, however, are clear indications of much good news among Friends. In numerous locations throughout the Quaker world Friends are thriving. Since Friends tend to communicate only within their segment of the family tree, these stories are not widely known.

As a sequel to *Among Friends*, Earlham School of Religion initiated a series of surveys of and conversations with vital meetings and churches with a goal of publishing the findings. For the purposes of this project, "demonstrated vitality" included influx of new participants, effective programming, and successful ministry to the immediate community while maintaining a clear Friends identity. This project had two primary goals: share positive news of worship and ministry among Friends; and create a resource for Friends seeking assistance with their own quest for vitality.

The School placed advertisements in *Quaker Life, Friends Journal,* and *Friends Bulletin* to announce the study and invite any meeting or church that considered itself to be a vital faith community to participate in an initial survey. It also sent letters directly to a few meetings and churches that it hoped would participate in the study. From those submitted responses, a group was selected for further study.

At the outset of the study, the hope was to have an equal number of participants from all branches of Friends. We had conversations with meetings and churches from Evangelical Friends International, Friends General Conference, Friends United Meeting, and Conservative Friends. Ultimately, no Evangelical Friends International church or Conservative Friends Meeting chose to participate. However, we received good response from meetings and churches in Friends General Conference and Friends United Meeting. An inquiry from a Quaker Worship Group at Sing Sing prison was a delightful bonus.

Meetings, churches, and the worship group were asked to select a cross-section of their membership to complete a twenty-eight question survey. This instrument asked questions related to ministry, theology, community, and business process. We incorporated these responses into a composite document. Members of the ESR faculty spent time with members of each group during scheduled visits. These visits ranged from a few hours to an entire weekend. The purpose of the meeting was to test the responses received from the cross-section of members against a wider sample of the membership. The content of this book was drawn from these submitted materials, conversations, and experiences of the ESR faculty.

The chapters here cannot possibly report all there is to say about these Friends. The hope, however, is to provide a glimpse into their vibrant lives and to describe it in ways that help Friends think about how to work toward vital worship and ministry in their own settings.

A few acknowledgments are in order. A conversation with Howard Mills sparked the idea for this study. Doug Bennett, (President of Earlham) helped frame the project in its initial stages. Tim Seid (Associate Dean of Distributed Learning and Assistant Professor of New Testament) and Phil Baisley (Assistant Professor of Pastoral Studies) accompanied me on some of these trips. They helped assess the initial responses, asked good questions of the participants, and listened well. Jennifer Dove-Isbell, (Coordinator of Annual Fund and Constituent Relations) helped compile statistical data into a format that could be integrated with the chapters. Finally, I offer heartfelt gratitude to each of the participating groups. The opportunities for dialogue and reflection they presented were, for me, enjoyable and edifying.

Without doubt, many vital Friends churches and meetings are not included in this study. Perhaps there will be future opportunities for making their stories known.

Jay Marshall
February 2005

Introduction

"The wind blows where it chooses, and you hear the sound of it, but you do not know where it comes from or where it goes. So it is with everyone who is born of the Spirit." (John 3:8)

As it is with the wind and the Spirit, so it is with vital meetings! A book that seeks to understand vitality among Friends brings to mind these words from the Gospel of John, which reports Jesus saying them to Nicodemus on the night when Nicodemus came seeking elusive answers to gnawing questions. A similar set of gnawing questions motivates this study of vitality among Friends.

While working with the data related to these questions can be as confusing as Jesus' language about being born again was to Nicodemus, like Nicodemus, perhaps Friends can understand that a relationship with God is at the core of the matter. The desire for such a relationship drives people toward worship in some fashion. The discovery and experience of a satisfactory relationship keeps them devoted to a particular style of worship. The key, when it comes to vitality, is to understand what constitutes a satisfactory relationship with God in the context of a community of seekers and believers. At the end of the day, the answer to that question will likely remain a bit of a mystery.

Imagine two churches or meetings located on opposite sides of the street in Anytown, U.S.A. Who can say with certainty why one thrives for generations and the other never does? Or why, with similar histories in terms of attendance, one congregation suddenly explodes with new growth while the other dwindles? Or why some people will drive past five other congregations of the denomination they consider their own in order to worship at the location of their choosing?

A variety of factors influence patterns of growth and vitality. A particular style of leadership or format of worship may be the primary attraction. A community's economic base contributes to demographic patterns as families often arrive and depart based on employment. These movements contribute to the ebb and flow of congregational life. Traditional family connections or the arrival of children may be a primary motivation for choosing one faith community over another. And, the rise and fall of congregations has a bit of a cyclical flow as well, particularly since recent studies indicate that most of what appears to be church or meeting growth is derived from persons *changing* where they worship rather than from persons *new* to worship.[1] Jesus' words to Nicodemus may be appropriate in this context as well. In addition to those influences, meetings and churches grow because the Spirit blows where it chooses. Perhaps that is the ultimate answer, and those who try to predict where it will blow next will likely have as much success as the local weather forecaster.

Creating healthy, vibrant meetings and churches is more art than science, and more divine blessing than blind luck. Still, by examining the experiences of those meetings and churches that seem to be thriving, it is possible that a description of vital meetings will emerge.

---

[1] C. Woolever and D. Bruce, *A Field Guide to U.S. Congregations.* (Lousiville: WJK Press, 2002), 46-47.

Each story may have insights that speak to the condition of other Friends. Looking at these stories collectively may begin to suggest qualities and commitments that, like sails on a ready ship, can capture the Spirit's wind as it blows and moves the group forward on a rewarding journey.

Nine groups contributed to this project. Three are unprogrammed meetings affiliated with Friends General Conference. Four are programmed meetings affiliated with Friends United Meeting. One is an unprogrammed meeting jointly affiliated with Friends General Conference and Friends United Meeting. The ninth is a Quaker Worship Group that meets at Sing Sing Prison. Each group has given life to the Friends' witness in ways that have been shaped by the forces of their local history and that continue to be redesigned by the current generation.

In the pages that follow, one chapter is devoted to each of these groups. Each has its own understanding of what it means to worship as a Friend, and each has chosen a set of emphases that shape the group's self-understanding. Every effort has been made to highlight the unique features of each communal personality while presenting each story in a format that makes it easy to compare one meeting with another.

Each chapter begins with a brief introduction to the meeting. The introduction is followed by a presentation of visible features of vitality that seemed most important to the meetings based on the information they provided. Next, a section called *Invisible Supports* describes the important foundations that undergird each group. These chapters conclude with a final section that offers insights into vitality that are especially valuable as Friends consider the subject and that could be useful as other Friends imagine ways to strengthen their meeting. Each chapter includes some statistical data as well. However, because there is no consistency among Friends as to the type of data a meeting should collect, a uniform presentation of this information is not possible. The book's final chapter offers concluding observations about vitality based on common characteristics shared by all or most of the groups. An appendix provides the survey used in this study, in the hope that other groups might make use of it as well.

Atlanta Friends Meeting
701 West Howard, Decatur, GA 30030
Southern Appalachian Yearly Meeting (FGC)

Established: 1951   Membership: 160

"Here we raise our Meetinghouse as a sanctuary and hospice, where all may be welcomed and affirmed in simple dignity, and where our children and their children after them may grow in their faith." Covenant for the New Meetinghouse, April 8, 1990

On the evening of the Atlanta Quaker Group's inaugural gathering in 1943, one participant chronicled in his diary that those present included "refugees, social workers, Friends, pacifists and curious."[2] This group officially met as Atlanta Friends Meeting for the first time on September 30, 1951. Decades later, much has changed at the meeting but the early description remains remarkably accurate. This consistency of composition is likely anchored by the commitment expressed in a covenant, written in 1990 to commemorate the meeting's move to a new, larger facility. "Sanctuary and hospice"--terms used in the covenant--connote a holy place for worshipful refuge and healing. "Welcome and dignity" create an inviting environment in which diversity is embraced and affirmed.

Architectural design and road signage each signal that the Atlanta Meeting is an unusual place. Sitting

---

[2] From the 1943 diary of George Hayes, as recorded in J. Ferguson and J. Rinard, *As Way Opened.* (Atlanta: Atlanta Friends Meeting, 1999), 1.

quietly along West Howard Avenue in Decatur, Georgia an attractive architectural design is nestled into a complementary landscape. The signs posted by the drive provide ample warning that this place of worship has its own unique character. In the best sense of space-sharing and cost-sharing, Atlanta Friends Meetinghouse also offers a home to other groups, including a Jewish congregation and a Unitarian Universalist Church. The Atlanta Friends School, which was founded with the help of several members of the meeting, utilized this space as well until recently. The building also stands out from its context in another way. In addition to being a testimony to simplicity and functionality, the meetinghouse is a well-maintained building on the edge of a less-than-stellar neighborhood.

As one listens to the journeys of the persons who seek community here alongside other religious seekers, a pattern emerges. One member has a background with the American Friends Service Committee. Another has a history of working for civil rights and anti-war protests. Another became a conscientious objector during the Vietnam War. Many Friends at this meeting share these types of concerns, making it no surprise that the group's involvement in peace and justice initiatives is important to its identity and to its members.

In this environment, a growing number of seekers find meaningful worship and significant community. A vibrant First Day worship is at the core of these activities. Reading and discussion of theology occurs each Sunday in the Adult Religious Education class. An evening Bible study meets weekly as well. Individual initiatives lead to activities ranging from mid-week meeting for worship, to starting a Friends worship group in surrounding areas, to sponsoring Friends in Friends General Conference's Traveling Ministries program. As way opens, the initiatives of individual Friends further enrich the opportunities available to the corporate body.

Visible Vitality
Worship

Friends have long contended that building structures are not holy places. They are merely the physical locations where people gather to worship. It stands to reason, then, that Friends will not feel a strong attraction to a particular place unless the quality of the worship experienced there merits such an attachment. At Atlanta Friends, the gathered meeting for worship has created a lasting bond among the participants and between participants and this particular space.

On a given Sunday at the meeting, arrival at worship launches a sequence of reconnections. Like extended family celebrating the opportunity to come together yet again, energetic exchanges characterize their greetings. A reverent buzz welcomes and affirms while trying to respect the needs of an atmosphere conducive for worship.

As Friends make their way into the meeting room, attendees experience something uncommon in most Friends meetings and churches—a crowded feel. Meeting for worship is not sparsely attended. The physical space here does not offer testimony to a faded, more glorious past or to unrealized ambitions. Instead, participants know they are part of something larger than themselves—a vibrant collection of individuals who experience the presence of God in worship as they come together in this manner and in this place. On many Sundays, nearly two hundred Friends and visitors settle into worship together.

In the early moments of the silence, activity continues. Late arrivals search for the remaining seats or stand along the wall. The usual shuffling of feet, sniffling of noses, and occasional whispers persist briefly before giving way to the weightiness of the moment. Within a short amount of time, the activity of waiting worship unites the group in the silence. Attendees remain diverse and free to listen to their own version of the Inner Light. Vocal ministry is frequently given, and reflects the diversity of those gathered for worship. Some express themselves in theistic language couched in metaphors of light, love, and nature. For others, more traditional religious, Quaker, and Christian language is important. Other vocal contributions will lack explicit religious language completely.

Within this gathering for worship, high value is given to silence. Words are unnecessary, as worship occurs in the spaces between the words. In silence, the busy pace of life slows for these few minutes. The crowded nature of the room disappears. The congestion of the mind and the smog of the soul have a chance to clear, giving way to conversations with the Divine.

Vocal messages will likely spring forth at some point during this worship. The variety of expressions matches the diversity of the group's members. Some messages are politically charged. Others reflect the headlines of the morning news or poems encountered in the past week. A few draw extensively on the Bible and seek to interject its timeless wisdom into this corporate experience. Many messages spring from the deep well of experience. Some wrestle with God about age-old questions that are never satisfactorily answered.

At some point during worship, children depart for or return from other First Day activities. While this transition may be mildly interruptive to some, to most, their movement is a welcome reminder of the full range of life that draws upon the riches of the meeting's family. Including children for a brief period of silence introduces them to the practice of worship without overwhelming them with unrealistic demands. Meeting for worship concludes with a handshake, followed by introductions, announcements, and news thought to be important to the life of the meeting. Fellowship over a cup of coffee or tea, or a monthly potluck lunch, provides yet another opportunity for a sense of community and support to thrive in this group.

Despite Friends' intentional minimizing of places as holy, the experience of worship within this group can elicit that familiar phrase "it is good to be in the house of the Lord." Worship here offers an exhilarating sense of calm that brings refreshment and renewal.

The act of corporate worship is the primary source of the Atlanta Meeting's vitality. Given their large and diverse membership, unprogrammed worship is probably the only worship form that could unify the meeting. What this group shares on a given First Day morning can be reduced to a short list:

- They share a common space at a common time.

- They share a commitment to seeking-worship within a religious community.
- They share a commitment to broad principles that are not rigidly defined.
- They share important connections with many of the persons with whom they worship.

Once silence settles over the group, the worshiper is free to worship God as he or she believes is appropriate. This type of freedom provides refuge from practices, language, and beliefs that some would find oppressive, even as that same language and belief remain available to those who value them. Vocal ministry is an occasion where one could have to listen to another person offer a message that is not harmonious with one's own beliefs. However, the commitment to *be* a diverse community and the fact that such messages will occur only occasionally make this a tolerable moment.

Ministry

Friends tend to define ministry in broad terms, holding that all persons are gifted for ministry of some type. This understanding of ministry exists at Atlanta meeting, though they are reluctant to describe many individual interests or projects as ministry. For these Friends, the practice of meeting for worship is the central act of ministry, both given and received. This reflects an understanding that these moments of quiet stillness are a collaborative effort. Their presence together is a ministry to those who attend.

Vocal messages, too, contribute ministry to their life together. Atlanta Friends describe this as a minor thread in the fabric of their spiritual life, and some wonder aloud as to whether vocal ministry is really valued. When such ministry is offered, Friends here expect quality messages of spiritual depth. However simple that may sound, a cluster of issues surfaces time and time again in the meeting. Quality of ministry is periodically a concern, as Friends seek a good balance of silence and spoken message. Choice of language can be an issue, as overt uses of the Bible or Christian terminology causes a concern for some. The use of worship for didactic messages of a political nature can be equally troubling. Popcorn messages, with too little distance between speakers are viewed as problematic.

It becomes clear that meaningful unprogrammed worship is not necessarily a simple accomplishment. Despite these challenges, the experience of being refreshed and renewed is a gift Atlanta Friends help one another experience by participating in this central act of ministry. The strength and direction derived from worship helps to prepare them for the work they will undertake in the course of their weekly lives.

When definitions of ministry extend beyond worship, those descriptions focus on activities within the meeting rather than demonstrating a clear connection beyond the meeting membership. When pressed to describe the ministries within this meeting in a single word, members gave several responses: community; God; silence; seeking; rest; support; worship; peaceful connection; Light; religious fellowship; spirituality; spiritual meaning. These descriptions seem to be characteristics and experiences the group ascribes to life within the meeting rather than specific activities exercised by particular individuals.

However, further conversation revealed that pastoral care activities within the meeting are shared by many, and Friends are up to the task at critical moments. As examples, members have offered care and counsel to breast cancer victims and have helped families cope with terminal illnesses. This is need-based care, with the expectation that it will be reciprocated as need warrants it.

Equally important in the ministries provided at Atlanta Friends Meeting is the group's support in members' discernment processes. Individuals bring their leadings to the meeting to test them with the group. As an example, one member felt drawn to live a life in which he was dependent on God and free to follow the Spirit's leading. After a period of discernment with the meeting, he resigned his tenured university position. He then began volunteering with a Quaker service organization, committed to living a life in which he is free to follow God's leadings.

In sum, while the concept of ministry may not be well articulated at Atlanta Friends, the practice of ministry is serving the personal journeys of it members. This is especially true in areas of pastoral care and personal discernment.

Outreach

Commitment to outreach also feeds the vitality of the meeting. However, it should be no surprise that the character of this outreach is indelibly shaped by the character of the meeting!

The case can be made that the meeting's commitment to diversity is, itself, a commitment to outreach that is ingrained in the meeting's identity at a core level. It offers a worship home, and in some ways a refuge, to persons who would not easily find acceptance in more traditional faith settings. This was true at the time when the meeting was founded. The inaugural participants included pacifists as well as some with a militant anti-Nazi attitude. It included persons committed to racial equality as well as those who preferred segregation. The meeting considered the issue of homosexuality in the late 1970s and early 1980s, reaching clearness to affirm such relationships years before many other religious groups began to consider the question.

Numerous social issues have concerned the meeting over time. They have protested war and worked with those who have been ravaged by its effects. Certain refugees, from Central America to Southeast Asia, have received Friendly assistance as they sought to rebuild their broken lives. The meeting even went so far as to adopt a "sister" meeting, El Sitio, in El Salvador. They have been actively involved in the American Friends Service Committee since the 1970s, and they encouraged the relocation of one of its regional offices to the Atlanta area. Members of the meeting have offered ministry in local prisons and nearby homes for the elderly and handicapped. They deliberately chose the location of the meetinghouse so as to locate the group near neighborhoods where outreach on peace and justice matters could have a local impact. Indeed, in the 1999 history of the meeting, the chapter devoted to social concerns is the largest chapter in the book!

This commitment to social concerns does come with an interesting twist. Despite a history decorated with impressive efforts and a present in which similar concerns remain important, most of these projects are individuals' initiatives. The meeting lacks a unified vision for social justice ministry and a corporate commitment to a uniting project. However, in keeping with the diversity of the group's composition, this approach seems to provide the necessary corporate discernment support that assists the undertaking of these individual projects.

Invisible Supports
Spiritual Foundations

Theological perspectives at Atlanta Friends Meeting run the entire gamut between fundamentalism and atheism, with a clear tilt of the scales toward the liberal side of the theological continuum. One implicit theological commitment evident in the composition of the meeting is the value of diversity and the creative tension it imposes on a group. Given this diversity, the meeting derives more commonality and unity from practice than from conformity of belief or values. Particular beliefs are seldom spoken of overtly in the wider community except during meeting for worship.

When Atlanta Friends do speak directly of the beliefs that unite them, the most common reference is that there is "that of God in everyone." Upon that starting point, Friends here believe strongly in continual revelation, *and* that this revelation comes via direct communication of the individual with God. No hierarchy of intermediaries is needed or desired. For this reason, unprogrammed worship is the most suitable format of worship for these Friends.

The concept of Friends as "seekers" is another important component of the theological mindset at this meeting. Truth is not completely known; neither is it limited to one set of absolutes. What matters most is that one seeks to know God and to discern how God leads.

Discussions of theology also indicate Atlanta Friends believe individuals are participants in community with God and have a personal responsibility as children of God. That responsibility begins as an obligation to listen to one another, though without the imperative that another person's words, concerns, or leadings must be taken as authoritative for anyone but the one speaking them. This responsibility as children of God also connects directly with the activist values that define much of the members' ministry and service activity in the wider community.

Vision and Business Processes

Business at the meeting is conducted in the manner of Friends. Intentionally non-authoritarian in their approach to ordering the business process, these Friends seek the sense of the meeting to make decisions. The group operates in an egalitarian fashion that carries forth the movement and leadership of the Spirit.

Committees play a coordinating role, carrying much responsibility for facilitating the work of the meeting. New initiatives are frequently motivated by individuals who respond to "fire in the belly." The meeting requires consensus before it formally takes responsibility for new initiatives, whether they spring from an individual or from a committee.

The meeting adopted a mission statement dating from 1990, but its contents are not widely known. The group recently formed a long-range planning committee, but as of yet, there is no formal articulation of a new plan for the future. However, it is clear that members imagine a long, natural continuation of the meeting with the hope that it grows and gives rise to other Friends meetings in Atlanta.

Lessons for Vitality

The history and experience of Atlanta Monthly Meeting offer some helpful insights into the issue of a meeting's or church's vitality. First among them is how deeply the personality of a meeting shapes its membership and its ministry. From its inception, this meeting has been committed providing a spiritual home to a wide range of spiritual seekers. Though open to all, it has leaned heavily toward the left of the theological spectrum from its outset, and maintains that preference even now. As a result, it is attractive to those who seriously desire a worshiping community but for whom traditional congregations have proven unsatisfactory. Their experiences and interests contribute to the shaping of the meeting's decisions about worship, ministry, and outreach. Peace and justice issues, including their early consideration of the meeting's view on same-sex relationships, are very much a reflection of the personality of this meeting.

For meetings wrestling with vitality, the question is not "should we be more involved in peace and justice issues?" The questions to consider are:

- What is the personality of our meeting?
- Do we seek to attract persons who are very much like ourselves, or are we interested in attracting a more diverse population? If so, what types of diversity are present in our community?
- Given the personality of our meeting and the people who populate it, what are ministries and causes we believe God is leading us to undertake?

This meeting also illustrates the strengths and limits of a commitment to diversity of membership. As a strength, Atlanta Friends Meeting models how a group lives creatively with tension. It has created a worship format that allows a diverse group of people to have a uniting experience. Given the many differences of belief, it places a higher priority on values and actions than on theological statements. These subtle moves are valuable ones for meetings or churches who want or need to thrive in an urban or multi-racial or multi-ethnic environment without isolating itself from the community.

This meeting also demonstrates that even diverse groups have boundaries at which point they threaten to become exclusive. For Atlanta, this possibility occurs most readily when strong Christian language offends the sensibilities for non-Christocentric Friends. At that point, toll booths start to appear on the previously free bridges that unite the group. The hidden boundaries will be different for other groups. Unless a group adopts "an anything goes" policy, it has boundaries at which point it ceases to be inclusive and welcoming of diversity. Vital meetings will seek either to dissolve the boundaries or to clearly acknowledge them as they redefine the manner in which they describe themselves.

One final insight this meeting models for Friends is the importance of worship as a time of renewal and discernment. This gift of worship is most easily visible in the language these Friends use to describe ministry at the meeting. Those descriptions gravitate toward metaphors of renewal that occur within the setting of worship. For some traditions, worship's primary purpose is to praise God or please God. Worship makes the top five lists of "oughts" that are pressed upon participants. Atlanta Friends is filled with people who worship because they *want* to, not because they *ought* to do so. The value of that type of worship experience in the midst of a caring community is highly recognized for its renewing effects on their lives.

Atlanta Monthly Meeting
Founded: 1951
Affiliation: Southern Appalachian Yearly Meeting
        Friends General Conference

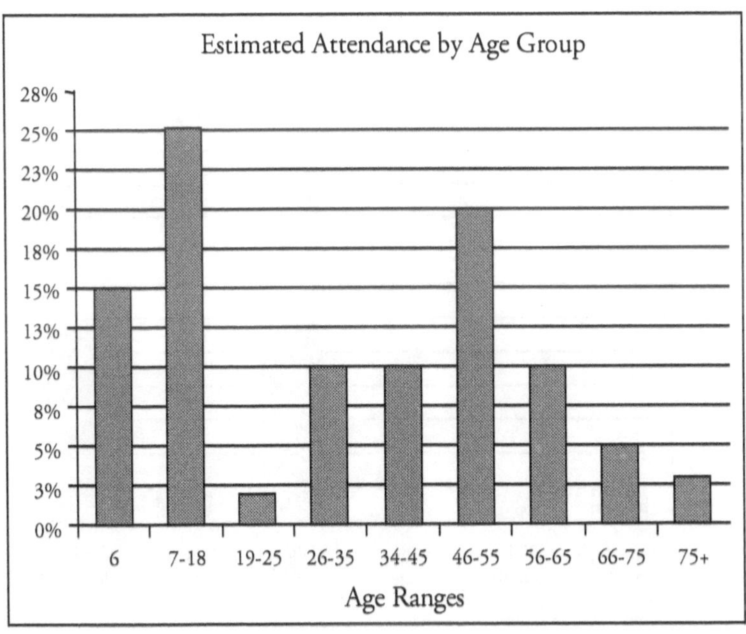

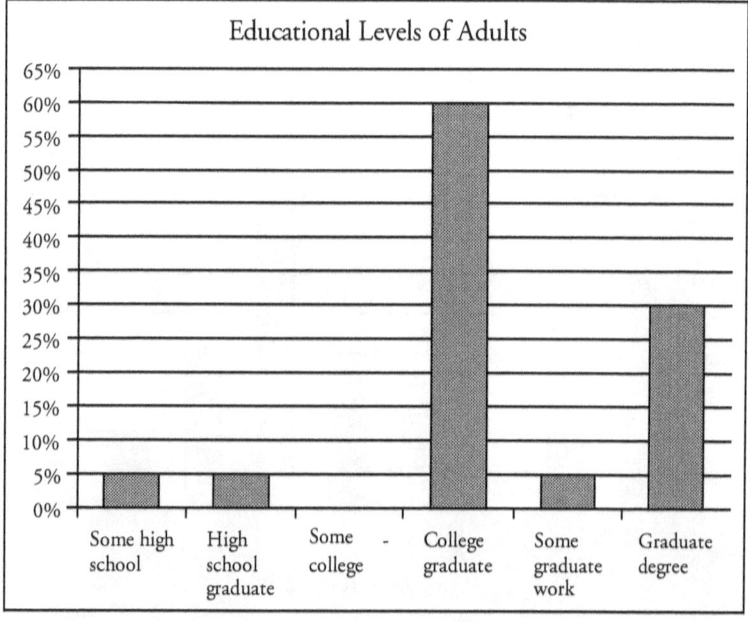
Educational Levels of Adults
65%
60%
55%
50%
45%
40%
35%
30%
25%
20%
15%
10%
5%
0%
Some high school
High school graduate
Some college
College graduate
Some graduate work
Graduate degree

Brooklyn Friends Meeting
110 Schermerhorn Street, Brooklyn, NY 11201
New York Yearly Meeting (FGC/FUM)

Established: 1975   Membership: 199

*"Again I saw all the oppressions that are practiced under the
sun . . . with no one to comfort them." (Ecclesiastes 4:1)*

The grid of New York City streets seems like an
endless maze of moving people and changing scenery.
With each approaching street corner, visitors never know
what type of neighborhood they will find. Business?
Residential? Ethnic? If those wandering visitors happen
to approach Schermerhorn Street in Brooklyn, a Quaker
meetinghouse will come into view. Located in the largest
borough in New York City—equivalent to the fourth
largest city in the United States—the surrounding
community is diverse ethnically, racially, religiously and
economically, and undergoes continuous change.

Though the Brooklyn Monthly Meeting was
established in 1975, Friends have been active in the
Brooklyn area since 1835. In 1837, a preparative
meeting was established here under the care of New York
Monthly Meeting, as were several other preparative
meetings at various times. When New York Monthly
Meeting reorganized itself as a quarterly meeting in the
1970s, Brooklyn Preparative Meeting was granted
monthly meeting status. Thus, behind what appears to
be a relatively recent date of origin lies a lengthy history.
In fact, the meetinghouse currently occupied by the
Brooklyn meeting was built in 1857. Decades later, a

rich spirit of worship and ministry persists in a neighborhood whose diversity far surpasses the differences that contributed to the Hicksite-Orthodox schism.

If community ethos shapes a meeting's worship and ministry, one should expect to discover here a meeting quite comfortable with diversity, where change contributes to vitality and enthusiasm more than to disorientation and dismay. Included among the members of the Brooklyn meeting one finds individuals with long histories among Friends, as well as former Mennonites, Episcopalians, and Roman Catholics, and many other journeys. The meeting contains persons of deep faith as well as persons who are searching for faith; persons with a heart for social activism alongside fellow pilgrims devoted to a deeply contemplative spirit. And of course, there are persons who embrace the ideals of both extremes, seeking to define a centrist perspective that embraces the strengths of several positions. In such a setting, respect for others will be essential; reconciliation of conflicting points of view and the hurts they can cause will be part of the basic fabric of worship and ministry. Somewhat surprisingly, one also discovers a keen emphasis on healing.

No one is spared from the need for healing regardless of the path they choose to journey. None escapes pain of some magnitude during their lifetime. Personal challenges can deteriorate into lasting issues that leave permanent scars. Social injustices often paralyze the soul of attentive observers, rendering the victims dazed and nearly lifeless. Spiritual unrest in the ongoing search for meaning leaves some in need of assistance from fellow travelers on this worthy path.

Though the need for healing is universal, the receipt of healing is not. This gaping chasm between demand and supply is at least partially due to an inability to find the source of genuine healing. Where does one turn to receive such a wholesome balm? At Brooklyn meeting, one effective answer is "a meeting for healing." In this case, a meeting for healing means exploring on a non-verbal, nonintellectual level.

Imagine a small group of prayerful individuals waiting in quiet expectation. Their seating pattern forms a circle, embracing a center that forms a symbolic as well as literal focus for their prayers. Two empty chairs sit in the midst of the group, vacant and available to any who desire to receive healing. Choosing one chair signals a desire for prayer without touch; choosing the other indicates touch is welcome. Termed a "Quaker spa" by some of its participants, this meeting is described as nothing less than "a blessing with hands."

Such a meeting for healing is available to Friends at Brooklyn Monthly meeting. Its story is important in a discussion of vitality at the meeting, both for the ministry it provides and for the process by which it came into being—for it tells much about the relationship between the meeting, its members and emerging ministries.

This ministry emerged from the journey and experience of one individual who happened to be reared in the Roman Catholic tradition. For a period of time, she ceased to believe in God, returning to church only when her children were born. Later she found Quakers. Among Friends, this individual encountered others who practiced and advocated for meetings for healing. Feeling nudged by the Spirit to take up such work in her own life and meeting, she presented her desire to the Ministry and Counsel Committee who felt free to encourage her to follow her spiritual leading.

Visible Vitality
Worship

Meeting for worship is unprogrammed at Brooklyn Monthly Meeting. Two contrasting symbols from outside the room help establish the mood for worship as worshipers settle quietly into this space. The first is a wonderful influx of light that streams through the meetinghouse windows. It lends warmth to the setting, both because of its visual effect and because of its deep connection with the way Friends describe the Divine. The second is barbed wire atop a nearby prison, reminding those who notice it of harsh realities such as crime, oppression, and punishment—the types of realities that inflict hurt and harm on multiple levels to persons both innocent and complicit. With symbols of hope and fear, warmth and heartache lurking nearby, Friends assemble for meeting for worship.

The meeting's primary forum for ministry and development of relationships is the Sunday morning meeting for worship. There, visitors feel the pulse of the meeting. In that worship setting, one gains a sense of the total identity of the meeting and of the fullness of their life together. Silence is deep. Vocal ministry arising from the stillness is rich, prompted by the deepest urgings of the Spirit or of the human condition. These words, delivered deliberately, give life and shape to messages that contribute to the worshipful communion already well-established in the quiet waiting.

Though it is unlikely that this one weekly occasion provides an opportunity for each person to be meaningfully and personally connected with *every* other person in attendance, the shared experience is great enough to allow each person to feel connected with the corporate identity of the monthly meeting.

How does such bonding occur? One key may be wrapped up in a story of a larger-than-life personality at Brooklyn Meeting–Larry Jaeger. Larry's name is mentioned frequently by persons as they describe their entry and introduction into the meeting. In their memories, Larry was an individual who excelled at remembering names and who made an intentional effort to greet people after meeting for worship. His knowledge of Quaker history and the frequency with which he spoke in meeting for worship identified him as one whose opinion should be sought and trusted by newcomers. To many, he exemplified Quaker values and process. Perhaps most importantly of all, he was available to those who called upon him. In this single character, one finds an understanding of the past, a vital force in the present, and a welcoming voice who helped to introduce and integrate new seekers into the existing social unity. In short Larry, and persons like him, help meaningful connections occur for new persons in the exploratory or introductory process of discovering a spiritual community.

Such a process is essential in meetings similar to Brooklyn–and perhaps to all meetings–because Sunday morning meeting for worship is the only occasion when the entire, or even the majority, of the meeting spends time together. If group formation and identity are to occur, they must occur here.

While Sunday's meeting for worship is the primary occasion on which members gather and the community is present at Brooklyn, the meeting offers several other opportunities, giving potential variety to the worship experience and also illustrating the diversity within the meeting. The meeting offers a weekly discussion group in a worship-sharing format. Those who enjoy music will find an opportunity for hymn singing on the first Sunday of the month. The meeting for healing, described above, meets on the third Sunday of each month. A mid-week meeting for worship gathers on Tuesday evenings. A Quaker-Buddhist study group meets monthly, as does a women's group.

Ministry

An initial discussion of ministry brings a clear message that ministry is the responsibility of all persons, but less certainty as to language and description of it. Terms like "ministry" and "spiritual gifts" are used with some reluctance by certain Friends at Brooklyn. The concept of a "recorded minister" encounters resistance as well. Much of this culture of suspicion is rooted in an approach to spirituality that opposes hierarchy among persons and prefers not to describe too much activity as a result of God's intervention. However, conversations with Friends here quickly reveal many activities that easily fit the category of "ministry" as traditionally understood by Friends.

Individuals moved to ministry at Brooklyn meeting test their leadings with the larger meeting, usually through Ministry and Counsel. Indeed, several exciting ministries connected with Brooklyn meeting originated in this way. In its recent history, the meeting held weekly demonstrations outside the New York State Supreme Court to end the death penalty. Outside the Brooklyn Borough Hall, a weekly vigil for peace started immediately after the 9/11 terrorist attacks. In the aftermath of that traumatic event, members of the meeting offered an escort service to the sizable Arab-American and Muslim communities in Brooklyn to help reduce their fear of traveling. Others participate in the "New York City Religious Coalition against Police Brutality." For use in these demonstrations, the meeting owns several banners that read NYC Quakers and include sayings from George Fox, William Penn and Martin Luther King, Jr.

While much current energy goes toward peace efforts, the meeting has a wider area of concern and attempts to fashion its projects to match the relevant needs of the moment. The meeting offers a monthly "community dinner" to persons in the area who need a free meal. Thoughtfully provided near the end of the month when bank accounts are prone to run dry, seventy-five to one hundred people are served by adults and children of the meeting. This ministry has expanded in recent months to include donated clothing and food. Another meal-centered outreach extended by the meeting is the Touch-AIDS dinner, through which meeting members minister to a frequently marginalized population group.

As an example of a different type of project, in the early 1970s, the meeting's focus was on the "Newgate Project," a ministry in which the meeting offered care for children of relatives wishing to visit those in the house of detention across the street. In many cases, lack of childcare made it impossible for families to visit their loved ones. The meeting ended this project only when the city agreed to provide this service.

In these descriptions, some important features of Brooklyn Monthly Meeting become visible. The monthly meeting itself is extremely sensitive to and supportive of the concerns and leadings of its members. It is important to note that support from the meeting does not obligate the meeting as a whole to participate in the ministry. It simply provides affirmation and community support of the initiative. While many important individual ministries exist at Brooklyn, Friends there find it difficult to rally support for, or even agree upon, suitable forms of corporate outreach that would involve most Friends of the meeting. This creates a setting in which diversity of viewpoint and expression can co-exist and even thrive. It will stop well short, however, of creating a vitality or unity that emerges from corporate activities that occur outside of meeting for worship.

While the meeting offers an incredible web of support to persons who feel led to a specific ministry, there is no formal structure in place to help cultivate or identify gifts for ministry. When such gifts emerge, they are the result of individual attentiveness to the nudges of the Spirit. The meeting plays more of a supporting role than an identifying role in matters related to ministry.

Invisible Supports
Spiritual Foundations

Brooklyn Friends unite around experience and practice rather than around belief. Systematic theological reflection, particularly with a goal of finding common ground among members of the community, is not a high priority. In the words of one member, "We are seekers. We are expectant waiters." However, discussion with Brooklyn Friends reveals some shared theological threads.

The belief that there is "that of God in every person" is by far the most uniting theological precept. These Friends are comfortable with the idea that each individual possesses the ability to know God within, indeed carries a spark of the Divine within. Seeking to know God and discern new truth or leadings is the core component of the spiritual journey. All persons, therefore, deserve love, respect and dignity. This, and the perceived value of meeting for worship, forms the foundation for this group's cohesiveness.

"Continuing revelation" is also an important theological concept at Brooklyn Meeting. This concept allows respect for ancient wisdom while it provides an avenue for seekers to discover, discuss, and embrace ideas from a multitude of sources. For example, it allows some members to regard the Bible as a holy book while acknowledging that it is not *the only* holy book. Likewise, it creates the possibility that some who embrace humanism more than spirituality or activism more than contemplation are able to receive and offer nurture within this meeting.

Traditional Quaker testimonies have some uniting power in this group as well. Simplicity, integrity, and equality all influence the meeting's identity, but the peace testimony generates the most activity. As the forms of outreach mentioned above in the section on *Ministry* indicate, ministry is more likely to be in the vein of social activism than spiritual nurture. Consequently, other values deemed important within the meeting are not explicitly theological or doctrinal, but are instead sociopolitical.

Vision and Business Processes

Brooklyn Monthly Meeting has a rich history with prospects for a bright future. It has achieved this without a clearly articulated, meeting-embraced, vision for the future. Once again, the memory of Larry Jaeger provides a fitting articulation of the meeting's attitude toward its future. One of the last times Larry was on the facing bench before his move to a retirement home, he stood at the end of the meeting and said, "Friends, I am not worried about the future of this meeting. I leave it in good hands," and sat down. After a moment, he stood again, and said, "I mean God's hands."

Trusting that God's care for the meeting is a sufficient long-range plan, movement and decisions for this meeting result from spontaneous and individualized leadings, and from the work of committees. Committees actually facilitate much of the routine work of the meeting and are frequently the source from which vision and energy for new ideas emerge.

Leadership and authority at the meeting bear the distinct imprint of Quaker ideals. Leadership is temporary in nature, limited to particular projects or term-limited appointments. The Quaker process is highly valued as a means of conducting business, though some Friends speculate that it has become a highly democratized process in a manner that is different from what Friends generally mean by "sense of the meeting."

Lessons on Vitality

The Brooklyn meeting offers some useful insights for meetings considering vitality. These Friends encounter and experience the diversity of this world in ways many Friends do not. There are still parts of the United States where the population is nearly one hundred percent Caucasian. In those settings, understanding diversity is often limited to learning how to interact with small African-American or Latino populations. In Brooklyn, this meeting experiences, and is to some degree comprised of, the level of diversity most of the world only watches on the evening news. As Friends grapple with the increasing diversity that shapes our society globally and locally, the Brooklyn Meeting illustrates one manner of celebrating and embracing change as a source of vitality. It demonstrates the costs and benefits of being willing to encounter the new and unexpected. One must take a lighter hold of tradition or single perspectives as the sole source of truth. An ability to engage others with respect without being threatened by points of difference or contention must be learned. The end result will likely be a much smaller island of certainty on which to stand, but a much broader and possibly more stable community of support can also occur.

A second lesson towards vitality that Brooklyn shares is as a model of a worship community for whom seeking is as important as finding. This is a natural companion to the commitment to embrace change. Because one is always encountering something that is new, it is to one's advantage to be alert, ever seeking the new lesson God may offer to teach.

An important question to ask when a meeting considers its location, composition, and mission is its relationship to the larger community. As communities change from one economic class or racial group to another, meetings and churches frequently discover they have little in common with their closest neighbors. Or, as congregations become entrenched in their own tradition or survival, outsiders may find it impossible to enter and engage with the people. Though still a predominantly Caucasian meeting, Brooklyn Meeting demonstrates an attentiveness to and care for the surrounding community. Many of its outreach efforts are designed to offer support and ministry to them without a pressure of proselytizing.

Brooklyn Monthly Meeting
Founded: 1835 as part of NYYM (Hicksite) and 1860 (Orthodox)
Affiliation(s): New York Yearly Meeting
          Friends General Conference
          Friends United Meeting

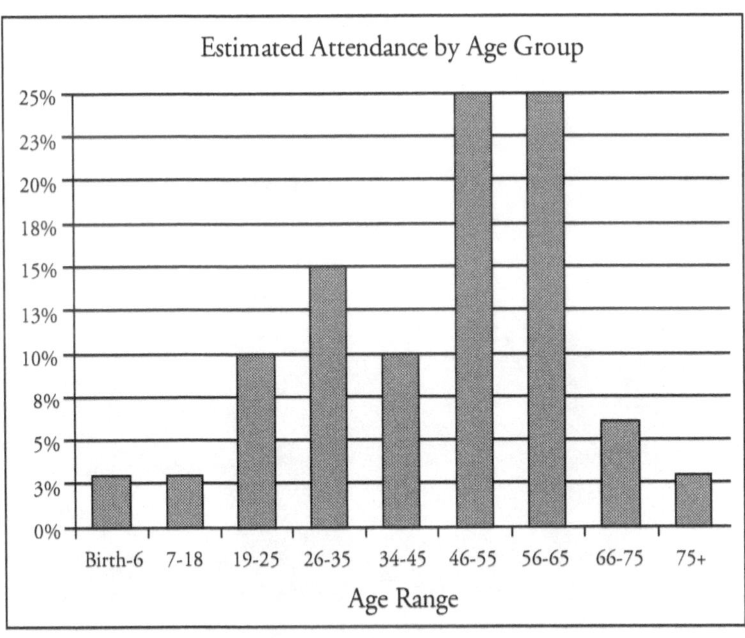

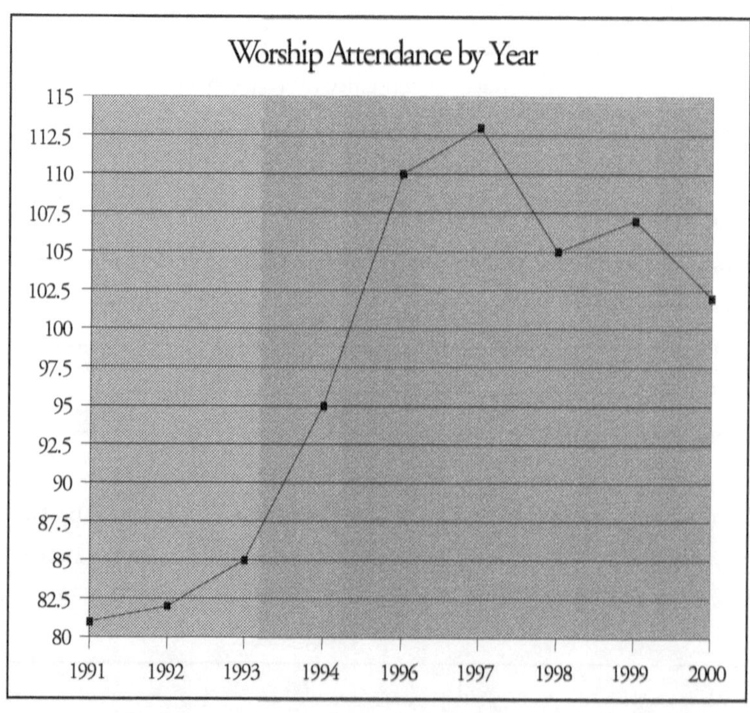

Worship Attendance by Year
115
112.5
110
107.5
105
102.5
100
97.5
95
92.5
90
87.5
85
82.5
80
1991
1992
1993
1994
1996
1997
1998
1999
2000

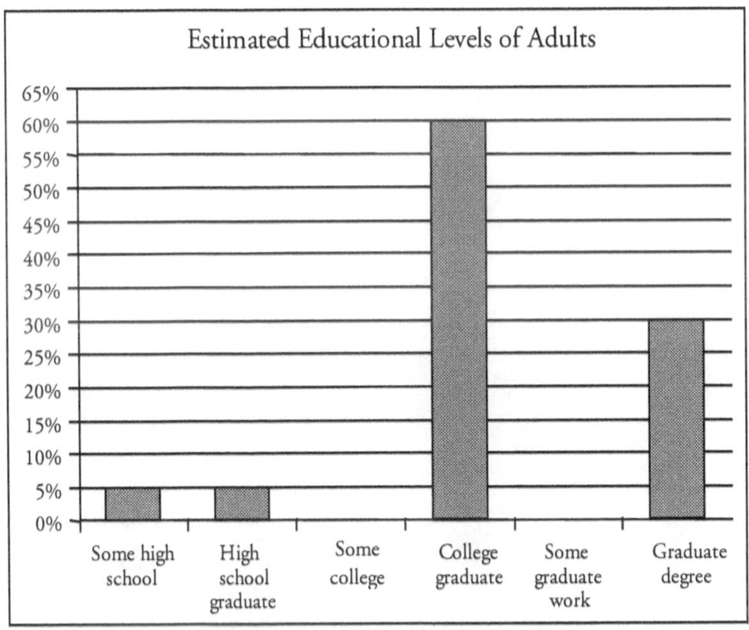
Estimated Educational Levels of Adults
65%
60%
55%
50%
45%
40%
35%
30%
25%
20%
15%
10%
5%
0%
Some high school
High school graduate
Some college
College graduate
Some graduate work
Graduate degree

First Friends Meeting Indianapolis
3030 Kessler Boulevard East, Indianapolis, IN 46220
Western Yearly Meeting (FUM)

Established: 1856   Attendance: 183

"We emphasize that true religion involves an immediate, inward, personal encounter with God, through Jesus Christ, and that this, rather than ritual and ceremony, is the essence of Christian faith."

Nearby highways provide ready reminders of the bumper-to-bumper life that accompanies residency in the city of Indianapolis, Indiana. Allisonville Road, Binford Avenue, and nearby I-465 provide daily passage for citizens as they travel for work and recreation. First Friends Indianapolis stands as a peaceful refuge amidst these automotive arteries.

Set several yards back from Kessler Boulevard, the meetinghouse's brick structure reaches toward the sky, towering like a safe haven for those seeking a respite from an often frantic pace of life. Its architectural design is comparable to Friends meetinghouses in the South, where structures depart from the more stereotypical Quaker designs known from the eastern part of the country. The building looks like a church, simple in design but complete with steeple. One of seven original churches in Indianapolis, Friends here have a long history of worship and ministry in the city.

Today, First Friends is an area-wide meeting with a largely commuting membership. Likewise, the personal beliefs of its members cover a wide territory.

Evangelical Christians worship alongside persons with a more universalistic orientation. A well-educated congregation, the meeting embraces opportunities to ask questions, challenge tradition, and wrestle with issues. The range of beliefs and questions fit comfortably within a Quaker meeting committed to a thoughtful, intellectually honest Christian faith.

On property adjacent to that of the meetinghouse, First Friends recently completed an outreach ministry known as "the meditational woods." Now, alongside the invitation to refuge extended architecturally by the meetinghouse, the meditational woods offer a similar opportunity within the beauty of nature. Though the project may seem unusual to some, it is a project appropriate to the setting, and one that addresses genuine concerns raised by Quaker testimonies.

Friends contend that all life is potentially sacramental. That is to say, God is present to humanity in every moment, and each moment can be an occasion of revelation in which genuine communion with God occurs. This understanding of God and life liberates worship from the confines of buildings and the activities that occur within them. It encourages recognition of the inward experience of God's conversation with each person. This recognition occurs more easily in peaceful places that encourage meditation and contemplation. These meditational woods were created with that hope in mind.

As in many large cities and metropolitan areas, morning and evening commutes to work and school in Indianapolis are slow, tense journeys for many persons. The northeast quadrant of Indianapolis in which First

Friends is located is legendary in this regard. Gentle reminders to relax, renew, and refresh do not come frequently enough. Places like the meditational woods provide assistance in achieving renewal when utilized for their intended purposes.

In Indianapolis and the surrounding area, acre upon acre of farm land is being developed. New shopping malls and housing additions accommodate consumer demand. In the process, trees, meadows, and open air are replaced by buildings, parking lots, and asphalt. Creative landscaping reduces the stark effect of the change, but nonetheless, the drive for profit overwhelms the conscientious objection to loss of green space. In a small way, in Ebenezer-like fashion, the meditational woods raises a small witness to the value of green space.

Though these woods are a recent addition to the ministries offered at First Friends, they provide a useful introductory snapshot to the meeting. This is a location where upper-middle class Americans in a midwestern urban setting are embracing Quaker values. Their ultimate goals are to serve God, find spiritual strength, and provide a Quaker witness in creative ways.

Visible Vitality
Worship

Opportunities for worship at First Friends reflect the meeting's efforts to accommodate the range of worship forms among Friends while providing exceptional care for its members. Predominantly a programmed meeting, First Friends also has a vibrant Wednesday evening unprogrammed meeting for worship that is attended by as many as thirty persons. Another unprogrammed meeting for worship occurs on Sunday mornings prior to other activities. These occasions for worship attract a small number of regular attendees who value the extended period of worshipful silence.

Immediately following Sunday morning unprogrammed meeting for worship, Friends gather for Sunday School. Four adult classes and eight others for young Friends and children meet each Sunday except during the summer. Another adult class meets throughout the year. Children's and youth classes meet according to age groups, whereas adults gather according to either age or topical interest. For instance, one class follows the *Adult Friend* curriculum while another group studies different books of the Bible, and yet another selects books that are recommended by members of the class.

Programmed worship follows Sunday School. Friends assemble in a room that exemplifies simple elegance. It is stately, but not ornate. It encourages reverence, but without the use of symbols.

A musical prelude begins as Friends casually enter the room and find a seat. Quiet conversation fades as Friends begin to center themselves in preparation for worship. The prelude gives way to a brief period of meditational silence. After a few moments, a worship leader welcomes the group, shares pertinent announcements, and invites others to do so as well. Hymn singing, Scripture reading, special music, and an offertory invite worshipful participation in a variety of forms. These are followed by an extended period of silent worship, typically ten to fifteen minutes in length. Described in the bulletin as "communion in the manner of Friends," it makes explicit Friend's peculiar belief that communion with God can occur without the use of the physical elements widely associated with communion in the Christian church. Worship at First Friends, integrates that belief into the structure of programmed worship. When the pastor senses the leading of the Spirit, he or she rises and delivers the day's sermon. When the sermon concludes, the congregation sings a closing hymn. The meeting for worship ends with a benediction from the pastor.

Sunday morning worship at First Friends provides the common ground where all members join for a corporate experience of worship. The meeting for worship succeeds in creating a sacred space without misidentifying the room itself as a sacred place. In the process of participating in worship Friends meet God as well as one another.

Ministry

First Friends Meeting embraces the concept that all persons are gifted for ministry. They look to their pastoral staff for leadership and a certain set of ministerial functions, but recognize that the entire body bears responsibility for the total work of the meeting. An egalitarian spirit shapes the business process as monthly meeting and committees strive to come to a sense of the meeting on all decisions. The practical effect of this arrangement is that there is not a single center that dominates the ministry of the meeting.

The pastoral staff provides strong leadership in the areas of administration, worship, pastoral care, and education. The majority of vocal ministry in the form of sermons and the visitation of members is their responsibility. Likewise, they oversee smooth facilitation of the wide range of activities. Leading with appropriate authority is well-balanced with participating as one member of a larger decision-making group.

Another strong component of ministry at First Friends is that of Christian education. As already noted, multiple Sunday School classes exist for youth and adults. These have great influence in the spiritual formation of participants. The meeting also offers occasional retreats for different segments of its membership, such as a Women's Retreat or Spiritual Emphasis Weekends. Such retreats promote self-reflection and growing spiritual awareness of God's presence and work.

Other organized activities within the educational life of the meeting bring together individuals based on common interests and life experiences. Traditionally strong Quaker groups, such as the United Society of Friends Women, provide fellowship and service opportunities at First Friends. The Movers and Quakers group offers young adults in the 22-30 age range an opportunity to enjoy fellowship in the context of service projects, discussions, or sharing meals. A Parenting Co-op offers child-care to families in the meeting in order to allow adults an opportunity to enjoy a brief release from parental responsibilities. Groups from the meeting, led by the pastor, journey to Costa Rica where they learn more about Latino culture while volunteering in schools there.

In addition to activities that have an educational or outreach function as a primary purpose, the meeting also sponsors several special celebratory events that promote fellowship within the meeting. For example, a Family Fall Festival, a Christmas Candlelight Dinner and Concert, a Sweetheart Dance and Dessert during February, and an Easter Breakfast are among the recent activities of the meeting.

The educational ministry of the meeting is well-planned and administered. It provides at least three important functions as the meeting ministers to its members. First, it contributes to the education and spiritual formation of its participants. Christian beliefs and Quaker principles are taught within these settings. Second, it provides opportunities for socializing and fellowship with members of this faith community. In a meeting the size of First Friends, these occasions provide for more personal connections with a sub-group within the meeting, allowing members' relational needs to be met. Finally, these groups frequently provide a form of outreach to others within or outside of the meeting. In this manner, participants begin to contribute to ministries of service that contribute to the Christian witness of the meeting.

First Friends understands the importance of outreach ministry and incorporates it into the meeting's planned activities. The meeting has created a formal relationship with the Peace Learning Center. In doing so, they lift up Friends commitment to peace and non-violent resolution of conflict. Some members of the meeting are involved in a prison ministry—a form of outreach that exemplifies the fact that the good news is for all persons, and that there is that of God in every individual. They also demonstrate outreach through financial support of particular organizations whose mission is congruent with the meeting's values: especially the American Friends Service Committee, Friends Committee on National Legislation, Friends Education Fund, Friends United Meeting, Earlham College and Earlham School of Religion.

Invisible Supports
Spiritual Foundations

First Friends Meeting successfully hosts the theological diversity held by its predominantly upper-middle-class membership. Members sense that values and practices provide their common ground more than beliefs, noting that the noncreedal orientation of Friends does not produce a centralized belief structure. The theological precept that "there is that of God in every person" surfaces quickly as Friends here begin to articulate the foundations of their Quaker belief system. In many cases, conversation moves directly to the importance of Jesus Christ. Not all Friends here heartily embrace the divinity of Jesus, but the Christian character and commitment of the meeting is strong. The teaching of Jesus combined with Quaker principles provide ample guidance for faithful living.

Integrity and equality are hallmarks of this meeting's expectations of faithful living. Peaceful resolution to conflict is also extremely important, though opinions on U. S. military action as related to a sense of national security reveals diversity and occasional strain around Friends' peace testimony.

While maintaining its commitment to a non-creedal Christian faith, this meeting recognizes the need to provide some self-disclosure of its faith identity and some guidance to those who visit their meeting in search of a spiritual community. To that end, First Friends includes the following statements on its bulletin and its website:

> Some unofficial statements are given below which will serve to give a general understanding of the Friends (Quaker) faith.
>
> - We emphasize that true religion involves an immediate, inward, personal encounter with God, through Jesus Christ, and that this, rather than ritual and ceremony, is the essence of Christian faith.
> - We emphasize that each individual has worth, dignity, freedom and responsibility before God (John 1:9).
> - We emphasize that worship is a personal and gathered community act of seeking rather than a performance; that communion is an inner spiritual experience rather than an outward observance.
> - We emphasize that moral purity, integrity, honesty, simplicity and

> humility are essential to the Christian life.
>
> - We emphasize Christ-like love through concern for suffering, unfortunate people; peace and equality must find expression in Christian service and social justice.
> - We emphasize the Spirit of God grants us openings, insights, guidance and understanding of spiritual truth consistent with the Scriptures.

These statements contain a healthy core of beliefs well-grounded in the worship of Friends: immediate, personal encounter with God; the worth of the individual; the value of worship in a gathered community; practical, social testimonies that arise from this experience of worship; and constant divine guidance arising from inspired sources.

Communication

Across the spectrum, Friends frequently have difficulty communicating their message. This can result when accommodating diversity leads to an inability to agree on what the message is. It also occurs when Friends cannot agree what means of self-promotion or advertising is appropriate. Sometimes, it is merely a matter of a meeting not realizing how much of what its members know and take for granted is not evident to others. First Friends Meeting manages to avoid these snares.

As an example of their excellent communication, consider the concept of unprogrammed worship. A person familiar with Friends history or with the unprogrammed branch of Friends may understand the practice of sitting in silence for an extended period of time, but hardly anyone else will recognize the practice as worship *or* know how to worship in that manner. To assist with that potentially awkward moment, First Friends provides this introduction to unprogrammed worship:

> For unprogrammed worship, as the silence begins, it is more fitting to settle into a reverential silence than to try to address God with thoughts and cares swirling through our minds and hearts. The Scriptures advise us to ". . . let all the earth be silent before him." (Habakkuk 2:20).

> **Center down in silence**
> "Centering down" means clearing the mind and heart from distracting thoughts, worries or cares, seeking with God's help to set aside anything that would prevent you from hearing God's voice.

> **Wait upon the Lord**
> Listen for God's voice within your heart. Seek to be quiet and attentive, focusing on God rather than yourself. Then open yourself to a thought, a passage of

Scripture, a prayer, a hymn, a specific concern, or to whatever else God's Spirit directs.

Be aware of others around you – their yearnings and needs
Be aware that they are seeking to communicate with God, too. Follow a leading to pray, either for the entire worshipping community or for some particular concern.

Add this explanation of unprogrammed worship to the description of unofficial beliefs and a map of the meeting house included on their website as well as in their visitors literature, and one sees a sustained effort on the part of the meeting to self-disclose its identity and assist those persons exploring the possibility of involving themselves with the meeting.

Vision and Business Processes
On occasion, First Friends has collectively worked on vision-related topics in a retreat setting. However, no formally adopted vision statement or strategic plan emerged from those processes recently. Smaller projects were undertaken to address particular issues that surfaced during these conversations. Even without a formally adopted vision or plan, meeting members share common ideas regarding the meeting's purpose and future.

These Friends describe their vision of the meeting this way: The meeting exists to provide a place where people can worship God by experiencing the Holy Spirit in a loving and compassionate atmosphere, and by experiencing one another's ministries. The meeting seeks to provide a community to seekers as it maintains a strong Quaker witness and a broad Christian faith that engages both mind and heart.

Within that framework, monthly meeting considers new proposals for ministry or wrestles with pressing moral and theological issues. In doing so, the meeting operates according to typical Quaker process. All persons are invited to attend business meetings. All have a voice in decisions. Within this process, the pastor provides information that helps the meeting think about issues, but without trying to dictate the appropriate decision of the meeting. In this way, the pastor indeed operates as a minister among ministers.

Lessons for Vitality

One of the greatest lessons modeled by First Friends Meeting is in the area of communication. Though no one points to communication as anyone's responsibility, good communication occurs repeatedly. It begins with signage by the roadside and continues throughout the meetinghouse. Even the website provides basic answers to initial questions of "Who are we?" and "Where are we?" The result is that First Friends is highly visible and inviting to newcomers.

The communication achievements of the meeting are even more laudable given the meeting's diversity. Rather than allow the diversity to muzzle their efforts to state the parameters of their faith community in broad strokes, they have found a way to utilize "unofficial statements" that begin to give form to a non-creedal

Christian faith. While not binding upon anyone, these statements describe their corporate identity. Meetings interested in vitality should not underestimate the importance of a faith community's ability to state who they are as well as who they are not!

The educational ministries for First Friends are described in such a way as to make apparent three important contributions a vital meeting makes to its members lives: education and spiritual formation; fellowship and socialization; outreach through service. A faith community that is not contributing to the spiritual formation of its members not only lacks vitality, but also lacks the right to call itself a faith community. A meeting that does not contribute to the relational and social needs of its members will find it nearly impossible to *be* a community. And, service provides a much-needed opportunity for a meeting to define itself through servant ministry. Each of these are crucial components of vitality in a faith community. The beauty of the educational ministry at First Friends is that they have regularized the process and engaged a high percentage of their members in these activities.

Finally, the meeting demonstrates how historical testimonies can give life to creative ideas that are contextually appropriate. A meditational woods, for instance, may have little impact in a rural setting where the Friends meetinghouse sits among pastures and cropland. But within a city like Indianapolis, such a project has both practical and theological value. Any meeting seeking vitality faces the challenge of giving contemporary relevance to traditions and values that its ancestors bequeathed to it.

Indianapolis First Friends Monthly Meeting
Founded: 1856
Affiliation(s): Western Yearly Meeting
                 Friends United Meeting

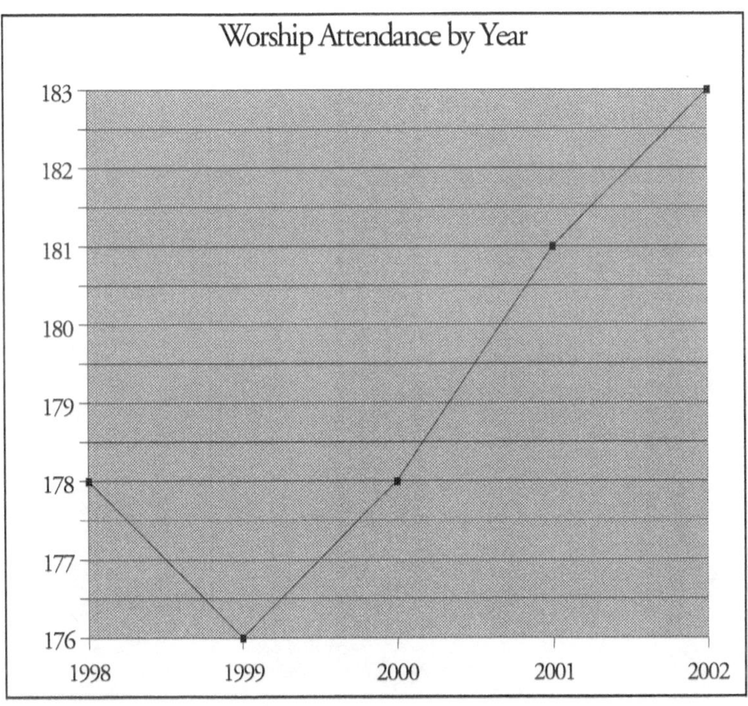

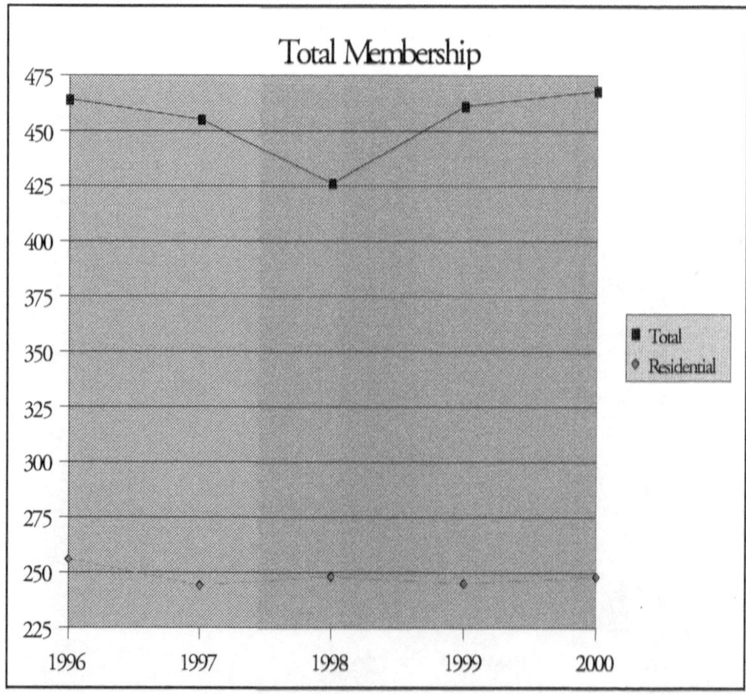

Total Membership
475
450
425
400
375
350
325
300
275
250
225
1996
1997
1998
1999
2000
Total
Residential

London Grove Friends Meeting
500 West Street Road, Kennett Square, PA 19348
Philadelphia Yearly Meeting (FGC)

Established: 1792   Membership: 351

". . . like trees planted by streams of water, which yields its fruit in season . . ." (Psalm 1:3)

A giant, historic oak stands guard over the London Grove Meetinghouse like a guardian angel keeping a protective watch. More than one person has been heard to say, "I hope I go before that tree does." Planted by William Penn himself, this wonderful oak tree provides lessons of presence, quiet strength, and stability to those acquainted with it.

Among the membership of this meeting, one finds a great diversity of spiritual paths that led to this gathering place of Friends in the shade of the great oak. Some members were born into this community and have been associated with the London Grove Meeting for their entire lifetime. A few midwestern transplants now call the area home. Some members came seeking a Christian or spiritual home that was more relaxed and inclusive than the restrictive traditions of their youth. Family and generational connections matter to many members. "Family, freedom, and lack of prejudice" are primary attractions here, as one member describes it. One friend says her presence here is a fluke, as her father was once a herd manager for a Quaker farmer in the area. Part of his job description was taking two women to meeting on Sunday. She has since made this her spiritual home because she found it to be "guilt free." Some came in search of the spiritual depth they witnessed in their ancestors, but which they themselves were not finding on their own. Others came seeking a faith community with a social conscience. Regardless of how they arrived, all choose to stay because worship at London Grove Meeting nurtures them and their life together is instructive.

Visible Support
Worship

Meeting for worship at London Grove is a rich experience in the unprogrammed tradition of Friends. The historic character of the room where Friends gather for worship contributes to this richness, as though an accumulated spiritual residue from prior generations of seekers seasons the atmosphere. Warmth and welcome combined with a quiet intention of seeking communion with the Divine define their moments together. A great variety of age and attire populates the meetinghouse benches. With assistance from Friends chosen to sit on the facing bench, together, they center for worship in the manner of Friends.

Some days, the silence is not interrupted with words until meeting for worship has broken. However, it is common for a few persons to speak each week. Members estimate that nearly one third of those who attend meeting for worship offer messages occasionally. Messages—some political, some religious, some anecdotal—are highly experiential, usually deeply spiritual, and reflect the diversity of the group.

The gathered meeting is an experience nearly all can describe with personal appreciation, knowing the power of those moments when the Spirit unites the hearts and minds of all in the most intimate of communion. Such meetings are not limited to Sunday worship; weddings and memorials tend to be occasions when the meeting is covered.

Though diverse in background and theology, Friends who attend here with regularity speak with one mind regarding the satisfaction they derive from worship here. Deep and rich, it nurtures the hungry seeker who longs to sit in the presence of the living God.

Ministry

London Grove approaches the topic of ministry with some caution, careful not to presume that too much merits the label of ministry yet also clear that a wide range of activities, undertaken in the right spirit, *are* ministries. As an unprogrammed meeting, the central location in which ministry occurs is in meeting for worship on Sunday mornings. This gathering for worship is a contribution to ministry, as every person's presence contributes to this spiritually nourishing experience; it is also a time of receiving ministry, whether from silence, vocal ministry, or the enjoyment of relationships with others in the meeting. Friends at London Grove place a high value on this key ministry though, not unexpectedly in a diverse group such as this, individuals have different assessments of the power of this ministry. For some, the silence is all that is needed. For others, vocal ministry helps keep them focused, and without it the waiting worship is less edifying.

Ministry at the meeting also includes a commitment to education. The meeting offers a thriving First Day School for all ages. It also provides stimulating educational events throughout the month. As examples, a recent Sunday evening discussion addressed issues of economic justice, while a film forum examined the life and witness of Gandhi.

Outside of meeting for worship, vital ministry at London Grove is consistently described as "other-centered." With a low level of both programmed structure and corporate projects, ministry occurs most frequently in the context of personal relationships. The ideal children's First Day School teacher is described as one who loves Quakerism, children, and the meeting. In nearly every avenue of ministry, emphasis is placed on being a listening Friend—listening to God in order to discern divine leadings, and listening to others as a means of understanding their concerns and needs before making decisions or committing to action. When offered out of love and care, even building maintenance is an act of ministry because it is done for the sake of others. With ministry of this type, nominal relationships make ministry less plausible. Consequently, members understand the importance of being present together and cultivating the depth of relationships that facilitate a ministry of caring.

Outreach

London Grove models the "let your lives speak" approach to faithful living, and is not prone to proselytizing the community. This approach has led to interesting contributions to the community.

One annual event that generates much activity within the meeting and the larger community is the annual plant sale sponsored by the peace committee. Begun years ago as a means of raising money for outreach projects, it was originally attached to a roast beef supper. In time, the plant sale replaced the supper. Each spring, the meeting grows or purchases vegetable and flower plants. On the days of the sale, the meetinghouse lawn looks like a Friendly Greenhouse. These Friends have raised as much as $18,000 from this project—funds that are then used to support a variety of causes. Work in North Vietnam, the American Friends Service Committee, Friends Home, His Mission, a local Senior Center, a local soup kitchen, and Friends Committee on National Legislation are among the causes that have benefited from this unusual fund-raising project.

Indeed, the peace committee is quite active, with diverse interests. In addition to the projects supported through the annual plant sale, the committee encourages letter-writing campaigns, offers cash awards to students for essays on conflict resolution, and sponsors a weekly vigil at the post office to give public visibility to issues of peace and nonmilitary solutions to conflict. And, the meeting has sponsored Laotian immigrants and provided sanctuary to refugees.

Even with these activities, a list of heavy concerns provides ample opportunity for future projects. For instance, fair housing is a concern, as persons drawn to the area for low-paying jobs have difficulty finding adequate, affordable homes. The issue is quite complex, and the meeting has yet to reach consensus on how it may constructively engage the matter. Aware that the meeting is primarily Caucasian even though the community is racially diverse, London Grove Friends have made some efforts to build a relationship with an African-American church in Kennett Square.

Invisible Supports
Spiritual Foundations

At London Grove, presence and practice matter more than words and beliefs when it comes to matters of faith. Their identity as an unprogrammed meeting in a non-creedal religious tradition encourages this position; the diversity of membership could not thrive without it. Particular beliefs are personal and are not frequently discussed openly.

When Friends at London Grove do speak about theological beliefs they share in common, the belief that "there is that of God in all people" is a core of the spiritual disposition in the meeting. For Friends here, that statement speaks volumes about human worth and potential, and it translates into respectful interactions and thoughtful engagement with each other and with the world at large. God is always present. Life is always lived on holy ground.

Building upon that Divine Presence, Friends in this meeting also acknowledge the Spirit's ability to do work through them. Whether supporting a grieving family during a time of loss, affirming an individual's leading to undertake a new initiative in Nicaragua, or offering leadership to a group that uses drumming as a spiritual exercise, acts of service, care, and compassion contribute to God's work as the Spirit utilizes their efforts. This points to an emphasis on personal experience as a defining force in spiritual formation. Through this experience, personal in nature but encountered in the company of others, Friends find their way to God.

Given their emphasis on personal experience, their affection for the grand Penn oak, and their attachment to the annual plant sale, it is no surprise that nature also plays an important role in the theology of these Friends. God can be experienced in every moment and in every place. All life, as Friends have held for centuries, is potentially sacramental. Beyond the mere experience of God in nature, London Grove Friends understand the practical implications of this belief: namely, that humans need to have concern for the earth and the environment.

Though not always acknowledged as "theological," the basic tenets of Quakerism, including its social expressions, significantly shape the spiritual perspective of Friends at London Grove. In particular, the Testimonies are frequently referenced as integral to faith as understood and practiced here. The meeting offers an eight-week course in Quakerism that explains social testimonies such as simplicity and integrity, accompanied by discussion questions designed to engage the spiritual journeys of those taking the class.

Vision and Business Processes

London Grove does not have a clearly stated vision that summarizes the mission of the meeting. However, meeting members operate as though the meeting will always be a vital center of Quaker worship and service while enjoying the shade of the Penn oak. They also possess a clear commitment to Quaker process that seeks to discern the sense of the meeting on important decisions.

Much of the work of the meeting is accomplished by means of an effective committee structure. Members of the meeting are expected to serve on at least one, and often two, committees. Four committees in particular play active roles in shaping the life of the meeting and the projects it undertakes.

The first of these three is the Nominating Committee. Within the context of the London Grove Meeting, the nominating committee functions as a discernment group that seeks to invite particularly gifted persons to serve on appropriate committees.

Secondly, the Ministry and Worship Committee is described by some as "the guardian of the meeting." It cares for the flow and details associated with preparing for and overseeing of meeting for worship.

Third, a Care and Membership Committee fills the traditional role of Overseer in this meeting. It offers various types of assistance to members when appropriate, helps reconcile conflicts when needed, discerns clearness for marriages under the care of the meeting, and maintains contact with members who no longer live in the community. This committee touches the lives of nearly every one in the meeting. Through its work, the meeting's care for and presence to its members is made manifest.

The Peace Committee also deserves mention in any conversation about vision and business at London Grove. Most projects directed beyond the doors of the current membership were either originated by the Peace Committee or are peace oriented. This speaks volumes to the tremendous power that this Quaker testimony has on the life and practice of the meeting.

Whether because of the diversity of the meeting or for other reasons, the meeting undertakes few projects or ministries that involve the entire meeting. Though the corporate witness of the meeting may be mild, the contribution of individuals who follow their leadings to serve is impressive. And though the meeting may not commit itself to the various projects, it does offer three important forms of support. For persons who discover they carry a concern, the meeting provides a safe place to give voice to the concern. Even if nothing occurs beyond giving voice to the concern, the meeting serves its members by offering careful listening and prayerful response. This is no small matter!

Sometimes, these concerns voiced by individual members will inspire the meeting to respond. As an example, the kindergarten housed at the meeting began with a member, near the age of seventy, who was interested in addressing a need in the community. The state of Pennsylvania did not provide kindergarten at that time. After careful deliberation, kindergarten was offered two days per week. When the time came to transfer the teaching responsibilities to another teacher, this transfer occurred under the care for the meeting. This kindergarten continues to operate at the meetinghouse, now offering two classes, five days per week.

Persons who believe they may be personally called to undertake some form of ministry are supported with clearness committees. When one member felt called to go to Nicaragua, the meeting assisted in the discernment process and ultimately agreed to support the member as well. A clearness process was again held when a member had a concern to attend the School of the Spirit. On another occasion, the meeting made a two-year commitment to meet monthly with a person coping with cancer.

This points to the third way the meeting supports it members in these moments: holding one another in the Light. Such prayerful support is beneficial during the clearness process, but is also valuable after clearness has been reached as well.

Although there is not a large, consuming vision for the meeting, there are mini-vision processes occurring in the lives of members who respond to the work of the Spirit within them. Admirably, those personal visions imitate the larger Quaker business process. They are articulated and discussed in the context of a caring community. Careful listening and discernment provides useful guidance. Friends are then careful to hold one another in the Light as they live their decisions.

Lessons on Vitality

Once again, this meeting's story emphasizes the power of the corporate experience of worship as one of the greatest sources of a meeting's vitality and health. In an unprogrammed setting such as this, there is no guarantee of continuity of content, but the testimony of the members assures there is continuity of satisfaction that arises from communion with the Divine. This experience unites diverse backgrounds and interests as the Spirit forges a commitment to the spiritual community that is formed in the process. There is no greater or stronger bond to be had.

London Grove Meeting provides a striking example of how a congregation can play a supportive role in the active spirituality of its members, even when the meeting as a body may not find unity to engage in a particular project. Their willingness to listen to the concerns of its members, to assist in the clearness process, to support the member who undertakes a personal call to ministry, and to hold this Friend in the Light during the activity is a powerful commitment to the spiritual growth of individuals in the meeting. Indeed, thanks to the diversity that exists in its noncreedal, nonhierarchical communities, Friends across the spectrum are easily immobilized around concerns that do not resonate with the entire group. This can lead to a perpetual process of laboring with one another with few decisions that lead to meaningful action. London Grove, while not entirely exempt from this dilemma, has found a significant resolution.

As a result of this resolution, the meeting remains meaningfully engaged in the spiritual journeys of its members. Meanwhile, members feel cared for and supported, and grow in their own faith and practice. Equally important, significant ministry and outreach occur because these members are released and supported to address the concerns that have arisen in their hearts and minds.

This process points to a second vitality lesson that should not be overlooked: the power of personal experience. Friends across the spectrum can agree that faith must be personal to be genuine. London Grove, more than any meeting participating in this study, gives specific emphasis to the weight of personal experience as a force in their spiritual formation. Certainly, personal experience does not influence in isolation from other significant factors. It is, however, a strong lens in the interpretive process that helps distill and understand the messages that are received from the Inner Light, from the Bible, from Quaker history, and from the surrounding culture. Learning to honor and celebrate personal experience, as well as to critique it, can contribute greatly to vital faith and ministry.

These two observations contribute to a third factor that contributes to vitality as well. London Grove shows a remarkable ability to adapt the testimonies so that they are rooted in tradition without being outdated relics, and so that they match the identity and personality of the meeting. In particular, personal experience and corporate discernment unite with the testimonies of integrity and peace, to produce creative ministries. Some teach a love for the earth while providing a service to community gardeners in the spring of the year. Others address concerns for equity and fairness to oppressed segments of the population. Still others lift up age-old concerns for alternatives to violence through the twin avenues of education and protest. Vital meetings will find creative outlets that introduce the transforming power of Friends Testimonies into the surrounding community.

London Grove Monthly Meeting
Founded: 1715
Affiliation(s): Philadelphia Yearly Meeting
                Friends General Conference

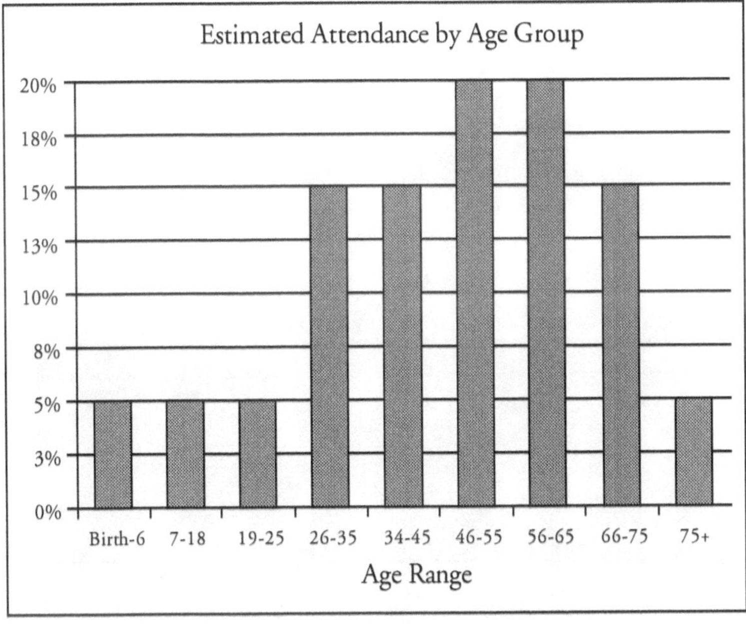

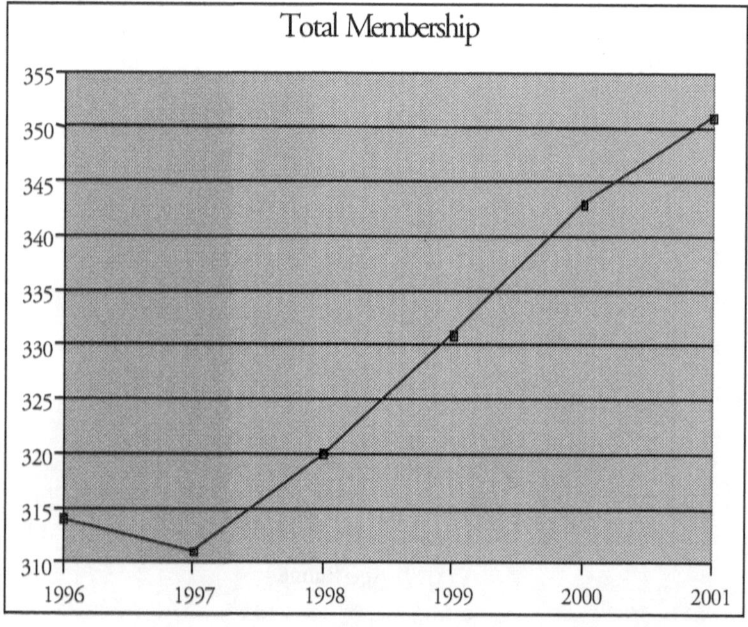

Total Membership
355
350
345
340
335
330
325
320
315
310
1996
1997
1998
1999
2000
2001

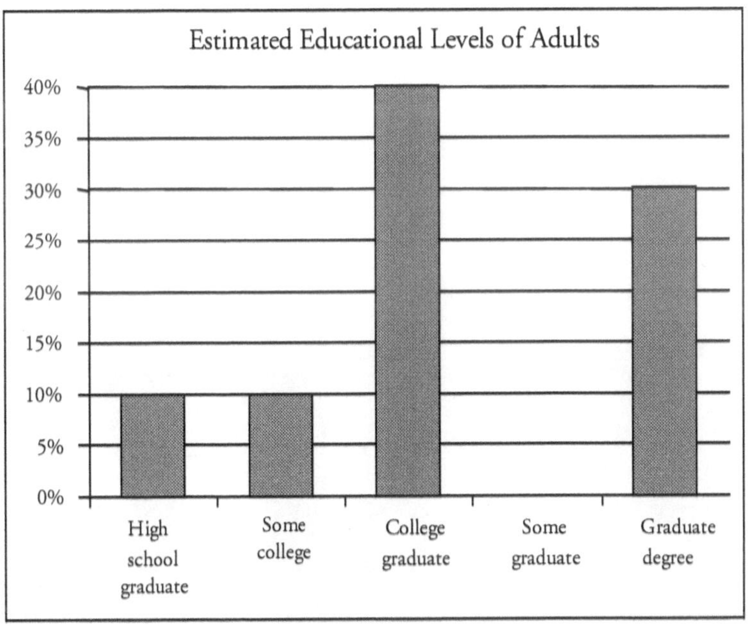
Estimated Educational Levels of Adults
40%
35%
30%
25%
20%
15%
10%
5%
0%
High
school
graduate
Some
college
College
graduate
Some
graduate
Graduate
degree

Newtown Friends Meeting
219 Court Street, Newtown, PA 18940
Philadelphia Yearly Meeting (FGC)

Established: 1815   **Membership: 250**

"And the lion will lie down peacefully with the lamb. . ."
(Isaiah 11:6)

Newtown Friends Meeting is located outside Philadelphia on a quiet, historic street in the small village of Newtown, Pennsylvania. It traces its origin to the efforts of renowned Quaker painter Edward Hicks, who appealed for permission to begin a preparative meeting there in the early 1800s. The meeting continues to use the original meetinghouse, erected in 1817 after permission was received to begin a meeting there.

At the time of its founding, over two hundred Friends transferred their membership to the Newtown meeting from other meetings in the surrounding area. When Philadelphia Yearly Meeting split into Guerneyite and Hicksite factions in 1827, Newtown identified with the Hicksite tradition, but was one of the first meetings to seek joint membership as a step toward reconciliation of the two yearly meetings.

The current membership of Newtown meeting is a well-educated, largely upper-middle-class group. Meeting members choose to worship here for a variety of reasons. Some discovered the meeting when they began searching for a place to worship, whereas others were born into the meeting over fifty years ago. Some counted themselves among Quakers elsewhere before moving into the area, whereas for others this is their first experience with Friends.

One contributing factor to the vitality of Newtown meeting is its close proximity to other Quaker institutions. Numerous other Quaker meetings are located within fifty miles of the meeting. Newtown Friends School, a K-8 Friends school founded by the meeting and still under its care, and George School, a boarding school for grades 9-12, are a stone's throw away. Two Quaker-sponsored retirement communities, Friends Home and Village and Pennswood Village, along with Chandler Hall, a Quaker-sponsored healthcare organization, operate in the area. Of course, nearby Philadelphia is home to numerous Quaker organizations, including Philadelphia Yearly Meeting and American Friends Service Committee. These numerous Quaker organizations create a context in which the influence and vitality of Friends is clearly visible, contributing to a sense of health and vitality for the Newtown meeting.

Most members of Newtown meeting describe themselves as traveling on a spiritual journey, seeking truth and meaningful worship via a tradition outside traditional Christian practices, yet longing for religious life that is also part of a community. Many found that answers to life's difficult questions were elusive, which led them to look for a place where, in lieu of answers, lives matched the teaching of Jesus. Some members are drawn to the silence as a means of worship—a format that works well for those whose experience of the Presence of God in life has taught them to look within toward the indwelling mystery. A less-dogmatic, less-restrictive understanding of faith appeals to these

Friends, as does engagement in meaningful forms of service that bring Quaker values to bear on larger social issues.

A brief summary of one Friend's account of his journey helps clarify this point. This individual has roots in midwestern Quakerism, and was raised among pastoral Friends as the child of a Quaker pastor and administrator. For a period of time, he considered entering pastoral ministry as a paid vocation. He credits theologian H. Richard Niebuhr with asking the question that began his move toward unprogrammed Friends.

> A seminary class in Ethics required a brutal exercise in self-analysis and introspection that sought an answer to the question, "Why Am I Here?" This exercise began to raise questions about whether or not a journey into ministry as a Friends pastor was the right direction.
>
> The writings of Karl Barth compounded the question. His thesis, as I recall these many years later, was that Christianity was a matter of faith. If you have doubts, you are not a believer. I had doubts. I could never get rid of my intellect when I read church history, the Bible, text books and so forth. Hence, I decided I wouldn't be comfortable in the role as a minister (perhaps as a teacher, yes) — nor would good folks probably be comfortable with me.

Comparative religion was one of my concentrations. I wanted to understand the compelling reason why Christianity is "more right" than Hinduism or Buddhism or Islam. Wars have been fought in the name of most religions. All religions have their perverse advocates. Is exclusivity and superiority a necessary part of formal religion? Does religion necessarily become bogged down in bureaucracy, protectionism, and self-promotion of its leaders— e.g., the history of the Roman Catholic Church. One reason I went to India for two years with the American Friends Service Committee was to try to understand the West and its culture and religion from a non-Western perspective. This was an instructive experience.

It seemed to me that the Quakers, and especially unprogrammed Quakers, had the best chance of avoiding some of these historic pitfalls — at least for me.

I also didn't believe an intermediary was necessary for me to worship, though I could see how such might be helpful. Therefore, I no longer believed it was my calling to be an intermediary/teacher/minister to others for their spiritual lives. I thought it presumptive. Hence, I stayed at Yale Divinity School with the intention of becoming a small college teacher/admin-istrator. The issues of the Vietnam War and civil rights in the 1960s (I returned to the U.S. and Philadelphia in late 1962) drove me into politics, campaigns, run-ning for office, and government.

These words describe a redefinition of the journey of faith. It not only operates with different assumptions, but also requires a different environment if it is to thrive. Once settled in Philadelphia, this Friend found that a strong First Day School, a commitment to sponsor a Friends school, and of course, location, all contributed to his decision to worship at Newtown Friends.

This story is indicative of the type of person who is attracted to Newtown Friends. The meeting serves well those persons who seek a corporate commitment to worship and fellowship without strict indoctrination. It encourages a mystical experience of the Divine without compromising the intellectual pursuit of truth. It values the outward expression of faith that demonstrates the connectedness of spirituality and practicality.

Visible Vitality
Worship

Meeting for worship is the focal point of life together at Newtown Friends. Rooted in the unprogrammed tradition, Friends enjoy a rich experience of worship in which the silence is powerful and vocal ministry is plentiful and meaningful.

Such worship is more than a mere gathering together in common space. It is also a sharing of a most intimate experience, described by one Friend as "soul searching" during which crucial questions are placed silently before God: "How do I live and move through my days . . . surrounding myself with God's peace and love? . . . What can I do to simplify my life? . . . Where do I need to work on forgiveness in my life? . . ." Such worship offers discernment of the life one is called to live *and* gives one the courage to do it.

A quote from the meeting's website speaks directly to the matter:

> "The place to find truth and inner peace is in your own heart and mind. What we offer you here is the quiet of our historic meetinghouse and the companionship and vocal ministry of other sincere seekers."

Ministry

Friends at Newtown easily discuss ministry from two perspectives: vocal ministry that arises from worship and ministry of service, exercised in numerous capacities within the meeting or in the community. Each type is an opportunity to respond to the calling of God.

In addition to the power of silence, vocal ministry is welcomed at the Newtown Meeting. Approximately a dozen Friends are recognized by members as frequent participants in vocal ministry, and several others speak occasionally.

While vocal ministry that proceeds from the silence is welcome and any person is allowed to speak, there exists a set of unwritten guidelines that define appropriate and inappropriate vocal ministry. Members of the meeting speak affectionately, though with occasional grimace, when they remember "the three Georges." Each George spoke every Sunday in meeting—a bit more frequently than is customary in the unprogrammed tradition. Some significant ministry occurred in those moments; however, this long-standing practice approached what some politely describe as "too much ministry." However in general, by weaving silent, expectant waiting with leadings to vocal ministry, the community gathered to worship experiences communion with the Divine; faith is refined and made practical.

The ministry of service plays a prominent role at Newtown Friends, modeling nicely what Friends describe as "universal ministry." The meeting has a strong egalitarian ethos, and leadership is shared by many persons. Assignments rotate from person to person. These factors—the expected involvement and the expected rotation—contribute to a vitality that arises from service while minimizing the likelihood of an entrenched order that occurs if particular individuals monopolize certain leadership roles or tasks.

Within this regular rotation, meeting clerks alternate between male and female clerks. An assistant clerk serves for two years prior to assuming the clerk's role, a strategy that provides the clerk with two years of "corporate memory" as she or he begins the clerking function.

Much work and ministry in the meeting is carried out through committee structures. Thus, the nominating committee's work involves discernment of spiritual gifts as much if not more than the mere staffing of committees and assigning of meeting tasks. Within this particular meeting, committees serve as the most consistent small-group opportunities within the meeting and become events for social gathering and spiritual nurture. In this context, the work of committee clerk frequently assumes more of a nurturing role than one might expect.

Outreach

At least three avenues of outreach make strong contributions to the community around the Newtown Meeting. First is Newtown Friends School. Founded by the meeting, the school remains under its care, with the meeting appointing trustees to the school board. The school maintains a commitment to Quaker educational, social, and religious philosophies. In this way, it is an aid to the age-old task of transmitting a community's values to the next generation of Friends. It also is a means of influencing the larger community: children in the school who are not from a Quaker background are shaped by this educational philosophy and the values that accompany it.

A second form of outreach is possible because of the strong Quaker presence in Bucks County. The numerous Quaker organizations provide abundant opportunities for outreach in the sense of contributing to life beyond the meeting, whether teaching in a Friends school, serving on the board of a retirement community, or volunteering in any number of projects sponsored by one of the Quaker organizations. As examples, in recent years, members of Newtown Friends Meeting have clerked Philadelphia Yearly Meeting, Bucks County Quarterly Meeting, George School Committee,

Newtown Friends School Committee, Mercer Street Friends in Trenton and Bucks County Peace Center. Members have also served as the mayor of Newtown and on the Newtown Planning Commission, Newtown Historical Association, and the Newtown Zoning Board.

One additional form of outreach illustrates the creativity of the meeting combined with historic Quaker concerns for peace. *Peacetalks,* a program aired on public radio, is officially sponsored by the meeting and an agent of the meeting. It is designed to challenge the violence that overwhelms and conditions our society. In the face of this reality, *Peacetalks* attempts to unveil the horrors of violence and injustice as the atrocities they truly are. And, the broadcasts also highlight creative initiatives people have undertaken to resolve conflict without resorting to violence. Stories from as far away as Japan, South Africa, Israel, and Palestine and as near as the Len'ape Nation have provided the substance and quality of this outreach. The talks seek to provide a counterpoint to the dominant paradigm of violence as a response to conflict, to help adults to shift their manner of dealing with conflict, and to teach children alternative responses to conflict and violence.

Newtown Friends are quick to acknowledge that most outreach comes from the efforts of individuals as they let their lives speak. Other than the Friends School, the meeting lacks a unified focus on outreach to the community. Still, their current impact is significant.

Invisible Supports
Spiritual Foundations

Newtown Meeting enjoys great diversity of belief among its members, ranging from Christocentric to Universalist beliefs. The meeting includes persons with Jewish, Muslim, Roman Catholic, Methodist, and Episcopalian backgrounds as well as individuals with a long family heritage of worship among Friends. Members view the opportunity to be part of a spiritual community without being required to submit to a particular set of beliefs as an asset of the meeting. Even without the persuasion or coercion of a creed, Newtown Friends identify several common bonds that contribute to their vitality.

At the core of their life together is the Quaker tenet that "there is that of God in every person." This fundamental belief provides shape to their interactions and depth to their expectations with one another. It breeds respect and fosters compassion.

Friends at Newtown also hold fast to the concept of continuing revelation. This, along with a strong belief in the value of the individual and to the value of listening to an individual's leadings, contributes to an atmosphere in which there is an openness to consider new ideas and give credibility to new experiences.

From this seedbed, Newtown Friends exhibit a commitment to seeking and supporting Quaker values more than to cultivating conformity of belief. Such an commitment is appropriate to, if not dictated by, an approach to religion that understands each person as a seeker on the road toward truth in which a primary objective is to experience the presence of God.

Yet another common bond within the meeting is created by the influence of Edward Hicks, or more particularly, Hicks' famous paintings of *The Peaceable Kingdom*. New members and visitors are given a reproduction of the painting, but the influence extends beyond this visible sharing. The sentiment of the painting captures the heartbeat of the meeting, as it seeks to be just such a place. People with different backgrounds, different aspirations, and different expectations are welcome to live together in harmony at Newtown. Indeed, this facet of community life is a crucial first step toward embracing the peace testimony so deeply rooted in the Quaker heritage.

Vision and Business Processes

Though the unprogrammed Friends tradition often fosters an environment in which planning and visioning processes are not priorities, Newtown Meeting is no stranger to either. Some in the meeting, however, suggest the vision lacks common definition and commitment.

The meeting still occupies its original 1817 building, but the structure as been renovated on more than one occasion. Decisions and projects of this magnitude are not undertaken lightly. As an example, a 1993 vision process identified the need for a building project and chairlift. Some eight years later, the work of that process reached fruition. The discussion proved to be long and arduous with significant disagreements at times.

Members can easily name a handful of other gnarly topics where disagreements persist and unity is lacking. Discussions such as these reveal the diversity within the meeting as well as their commitment to the ideals of the peaceable kingdom and to one another.

Lessons on Vitality

Quakers as a whole are a small, decentralized group. Ordinarily, they closely guard their autonomy and their privacy. One consequence of this is that Friends sometimes forget the value of connections with the larger universe of Quaker causes. Realistically, some Friends live in areas where there are no constant, visible reminders of that community. Newtown Meeting provides a helpful example of the reciprocal vitality that can occur when Friends find ways to maintain meaningful connections with one another.

The experience of worship in a community should, by virtue of its dynamics, create intimacy among the members of the community. Intimacy requires honesty, compassion, and a willingness to be vulnerable. In all likelihood, an intimate spiritual community will be possessed by a certain fragility. Only those meetings or churches populated by individuals who are willing to invest in the continuous, and sometimes difficult, work of tending to these relationships will remain vital. Newtown Friends nicely models this type of attentive care.

This meeting also demonstrates the value of understanding one's own corporate identity and the value of disclosing that identity. Of course, this requires that members of a meeting invest the time and effort into thinking about the issues of their purpose and objectives as a meeting. People attend a meeting for a variety of reasons. Once a certain level of comfort is achieved, they are likely to remain there. Many meetings and churches contain a range of diversity among its members, not because they sought to be diverse but because an organic amalgamation occurred over time. Not all congregations are comfortable with this lack of conformity. Newtown is able to say openly that it contains persons for whom Christ is important as well as persons whose religious practice does not depend upon traditional Christian concepts. Such comfort or lack thereof contributes directly to a meeting's or church's ability to labor patiently and respectfully during conflict. It also affects the range of projects they will be able to envision, adopt and support as a meeting. The clearer a meeting can be about its identity and purpose, the better it can serve the discernment process of those who come seeking community for worship and spiritual growth.

Newtown Monthly Meeting
Founded: 1815
Affiliation(s): Philadelphia Yearly Meeting
                 Friends General Conference

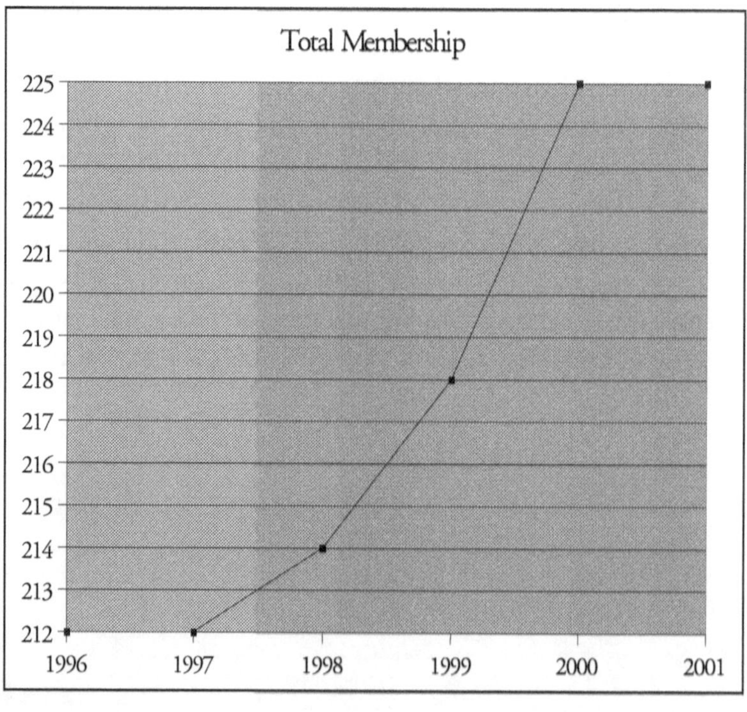

Riverside Friends Church
527 North Kentucky Avenue, Iowa 50402
Iowa Yearly Meeting (FUM)

Established: 1979   Membership: 72

"And a sower went out to sow . . ." (Matthew 13:3)

The surrounding area is reminiscent of a lush, park setting—the kind of place a family visits for a Sunday picnic and afternoon of renewal. This is the home of Riverside Friends Church, located along the beautiful Winnebago River in Mason City, Iowa. Established in 1979, Riverside Friends was planted by Honey Creek-New Providence Friends Church of Iowa Yearly Meeting.

Its members represent a diverse background of religious experience within the Christian tradition. Some have previous affiliations with Friends and consider that connection to be an important part of their spiritual home. Others came seeking a family church with a strong mission orientation. Some were from charismatic and Pentecostal backgrounds, and were seeking a similar worship experience in their new faith community. The pastor is most recently from the Open Bible tradition but has become a recorded Friends pastor.

Though started by Friends, the connection with a Quaker sense of identity is not particularly strong. Geographical location in northern Iowa and the accompanying isolation contribute to this fact, though the pastor is working to develop greater involvement with Iowa Yearly Meeting. Camp for youth, awareness of mission opportunities, and involvement with the United Society of Friends Women are providing opportunities for building relationships. Even so, the primary focus of Riverside's mission is on creating and nurturing personal relationships with Jesus Christ.

One can hardly argue that the seeds being sown in ministry here are not bearing fruit. On a typical Sunday, an attorney worships alongside a man he once helped send to prison. Business suits and blue jeans are both welcomed attire. The congregation heeds James' admonishment against being a respecter of persons that honors meaningless social stratification. From experience come testimonies such as these:

- "I attend to honor God, to come together with others who desire God's presence, and to get marching orders." —*Government Employee*
- "They teach and show the love of Jesus." —*Day Care Provider*
- "The people accept you as you are and encourage you to be all you can be in Christ." — *Attorney*
- "No one complains about my long hair and earring." —*Anonymous*
- "We have a great resource, the prayer chain, to reach others in time of need." — *Factory Worker*

Different social and economic backgrounds sing together. They struggle together. They fellowship together. They grow together. Welcome to Riverside Friends Church, where faith looks a bit radical among the landscape of Friends, but where God is changing lives.

Visible Vitality
Worship

Gather a group of the Riverside Friends into a conversation about worship and ministry and vitality will begin to percolate like a geyser preparing to gush. Enthusiasm and energy abound when these Friends converse. This is true whether they are reminiscing about past ministry efforts or collaborating on their next project.

Riverside Friends' visitor literature states "<u>We're Here to H.E.L.P.</u>" "Help" is an acronym for:

> <u>H</u>onor God
> <u>E</u>quip Believers
> <u>L</u>ove People
> <u>P</u>ray Fervently

Honoring God and equipping believers accurately describes their understanding of the act of worship. Loving people and praying fervently undergird their evangelistic outreach.

The act of worship at Riverside Friends has two primary purposes. First, to praise and glorify God. Second, to hold persons accountable in the presence of God as a means of equipping believers for the work at hand. Following an opening prayer, announcements and an offering, the congregation enters a period of praise and worship. Their music can be loud. It can be up-tempo. It must be directed at praising and honoring

God. This period of praise and worship is followed by a period of silent worship. Though rooted in the traditional practices of Friends, the period is frequently filled with testimonies of God's presence and work in the lives of the speakers. Following the testimonies, the pastor delivers a sermon.

Worship at Riverside Friends is rooted in the belief of the power of God to change lives. In this congregation one finds an interesting mix of traditional Quaker concepts with charismatic practices. Drums, rock and roll music, and praise bands contribute to the Sunday worship and provide opportunities for members to glorify God and minister to the group while setting a worshipful context for those present. The gift of speaking in tongues is also practiced.

Alongside these up-tempo elements, silence is an integral part of worship at Riverside. Great emphasis is given to learning to be still, and to being stilled by the Spirit. Silence gives rise to the Spirit and messages emerge from the silence. This seems to be a case where silence is properly the means to an end rather than a medium of worship that is, itself, revered. This is silence where people wait upon God with the understanding that the power of God can change the human heart, redeem the human life, and reconcile human relationships.

Friends at Riverside emphasize a commitment to accept people as they are; however great emphasis is placed upon accountability. Professions of faith lead to new expectations in how one lives. Commitment to Christ requires acknowledging his Lordship and submitting one's life to Jesus. All persons may come as they are, but they may not stay as they are for discipleship introduces radical change into the lives of all who believe. The process of worshiping together and growing in discipleship together creates the vital community these Friends share.

Outreach

Winning persons to Christ is a major emphasis for Riverside Friends. Such an emphasis would be affirmed by many evangelical churches. At Riverside, this commitment is more than theory. It goes beyond the wishes of the pastor. It is embraced by the membership, to a person, it seems. Consequently, evangelistic concerns permeate church planning.

The words of a former mentor continue to frame the pastor's leadership relative to evangelism: "There are two ways to reach people. You can either throw a party, or crash someone else's party." Throwing parties can require lots of funding, so Riverside makes a practice of crashing parties already planned by others, and is creative and courageous in doing so.

Like many small midwestern towns whose economic base has disintegrated with time, Mason City has sought to be creative as it generates new revenue. One major event that has wide city support is the annual Band Festival, commemorating the city's ties to Meredith Willson, author of *Music Man*. The festival includes a parade that attracts as many as ten thousand people.

The members of Riverside Friends view this event as an opportunity for evangelism—ten thousand people arrive a couple of hours early in order to look for a good location from which to watch the parade activities. Once they have found a place, they stay put for fear of losing it.

How might Riverside Friends capitalize on this opportunity for sharing the gospel to this ready-made audience?

The group begins the day before the event, walking the route of the parade, praying as they proceed. If they are to succeed, it will be because God has prepared the hearers' hearts for the seed they will sow.

As the crowd arrives, Friends distribute evangelistic tracts all along the route—"Dear Friend, We want you to know Jesus loves you . . ." Those who distribute the tracts offer verbal testimony to accompany the written words they give away.

Later, other members of the church walk the route, preaching the gospel. As they do so, children distribute stickers to other children in the crowd and utilize those moments to share the Good News.

Some years, Riverside Friends even enter the parade's float contest and share their love for music. As their float makes its way along the route, their band performs familiar songs to which they have substituted Christian lyrics. Besides being an activity the band greatly enjoys, the music puts the Gospel message before the crowd one more time that day.

The evangelistic activity of Riverside Friends is not limited to Mason City. One of the more fascinating evangelism projects involved their decision to witness at an outdoor rock and roll concert called "Moon Dance." Held in Minnesota, the concert involved several bands inside a fenced compound. Riverside Friends, in partnership with other churches from Walker, Minnesota decided to set up their own concert area across the road from this one. However, the promoters actually invited Riverside Friends to play inside their compound.

Once inside, the promoters assigned them a location on the path to the rock bands. This would seem to be a less than optimal location that might discourage less creative people, but Riverside Friends capitalized on the moment. They erected their stage there. Anticipating that many intoxicated individuals would be walking by on their way back to their campers at some point during the night, they decided to be prepared. They brewed fresh coffee and had an ample supply of five gallon buckets available. Their band played.

The party continued as concert attenders came to their location. Many observers played along with the band, using one of the buckets as a personal drum. Others used the buckets as a receptacle for their vomit as the activities of the evening began to catch up with them. A few Friends were available to offer coffee and to pray with those who, in this moment, sensed their life needed a change.

The members of Riverside Friends are quite honest in their assessment of these activities. They do not know how frequently their efforts lead to sustained change and a meaningful, lasting relationship with Christ. Things can look much different in the morning. They are certain, however, that their role in the matter is to be faithful. In this case, it means sowing the seed in creative ways.

With creative ideas such as these, Riverside Friends have offered outreach ministries at places like these:

Mardi Gras	Angel Tree Ministry
Soup Kitchens	Moon Dance
Music Man Square	Local Campgrounds
Walk Around Minnesota	Local Nursing
Homes Chicago	Opportunity Village
4th of July Celebrations	Appalachia
NYC Ground Zero	Albuquerque
Mexico	

Ministry

Ministry at Riverside Friends is a responsibility jointly shared by all the members. The pastor is an authoritative figure and has significant influence in planning church activities. However, all members have the opportunity to share their ideas and voice their concerns. A consultative attitude frames their work together.

This church teaches members how to minister through modeling the practice of ministry and through including new members in processes of discernment. This method of promoting ministry begins with the pastor, who models a collaborative approach to ministry both in his planning style and in his manner of participation. He prays openly about his personal ministry. He prays corporately with the group, seeking guidance for their collective ministry. He is willing to voice ideas and strategies as suggestions for group consideration, while he demonstrates an openness to challenge and a willingness to be convinced that ideas other than his own are the ones God desires for the next project.

Members of Riverside seem to embrace the idea that ministry is the responsibility of all persons. Once a planning session is completed, the weight of an approved project does not become a burdensome yoke for one person. Though levels of activity by all persons will vary in any given project, the entire group embraces the project and feels a sense of ownership for it. To some degree, all will participate by giving their time, resources, and prayer to the topic.

Modeling ministry extends to the children of the church as well. Perhaps more than any other group interviewed in this project, members of Riverside Friends do more than simply teach their children the biblical stories. They also involve them with ministry, particularly with evangelistic activities. When the church undertakes an evangelistic initiative, the children have roles to fill as well. This may mean participation in the prayer activities related to the event. Or, it may involve their sharing the gospel as well. For the band festival, a member taught them to share the gospel by means of salvation bracelets. As adults model this expression of faith, the children are included so that they, too, develop a confident commitment in their lives as a witness to Christ.

Invisible Supports
Spiritual Foundations

Riverside Friends operates with fairly traditional Christian theology. Among Friends, their charismatic tendencies make them distinct, as that feature is not common among North American Friends. Even so, their beliefs and practices possess some strong similarities with first-generation Friends.

Jesus Christ is the living center of the belief system that sustains Riverside Friends. God is Sovereign over all creation. All their activities point to the necessity of a personal, saving relationship with Jesus Christ as Lord and Savior. This relationship is openly acknowledged, and includes more than mere verbal confession. Friends at Riverside expect one another's lives to be living testimonies that bear witness to Jesus. This includes taking responsibility for reaching out to others, whether to visitors in worship or to strangers on street corners.

The immediacy of the Holy Spirit is important in the belief system at Riverside. People can know the power of the Spirit through worship in silence. They wait upon the power of the Lord, much as early Friends did, and expect the Spirit to convict them of their sins, grant them direction, or give them vocal ministry to share. Speaking in tongues is accepted as part of the Holy Spirit's movement among them.

These experiences weave together to create a sense of "standard of living." This is not expressed as doctrines or creeds, but it does translate into a genuine commitment to mutual accountability. Lives change when confronted with the power of God. Persons who accept Christ as Savior are expected to live lives that reflect their experience of the Holy Spirit's works. Unwanted habits and sinful attitudes begin to disappear—some easily and some only with tremendous struggle. New expectations and standards belong in the lives of the redeemed, and continue to form as Christians experience the Holy Spirit.

Community

Riverside Friends is, in the best sense of the term, "in the world but not of it." They live, work, and shop in the typical locations. They rub shoulders with Christians and non-Christians on a regular basis. Indeed, they seek contact with unbelievers, for those encounters bring moments of ministry to fruition. The community is, indeed, the field for the harvest. Anyone who does not know Jesus is either a field ready for sowing or a fruit ripe for the picking. Only active engagement reveals which is the case.

For this model of living to have integrity, members of Riverside need to have a strong commitment to God through Christ and to the standards of living they equate with a genuine confession of faith.

As noted by their outreach projects, most encounters are overtly evangelistic in which they proclaim the message of Christ, call persons to consider the Truth, and perhaps, to make a decision. There are, however, some projects that address immediate physical and emotional needs. The soup kitchen or angel tree projects are examples of ministry that meets physical needs even while seeking to make a spiritual connection.

Vision and Business Processes

Though the pastor has a strong influence in decision- making and in the vision of the congregation, the entire church participates in corporate discernment and decision making. A consensus emerges as the group labors together. Vision for new initiatives comes from decision-making and vision-casting at Riverside is, frankly, a pleasant surprise. An annual retreat provides a significant opportunity for fellowship, planning, and discernment.

Lessons on Vitality

Once again, this meeting reminds Friends of the value of clarity of purpose. Every meeting has limited time and resources. A meeting can choose to focus upon any number of initiatives, but it cannot make *every* initiative a priority no matter how valuable the initiative may be. Riverside Friends benefits from their clear sense of purpose. Unlike many mission statements that simply fade on the paper upon which they are written, Riverside lives its mission. Meetings that cannot achieve clarity of purpose will likely hobble half their effectiveness by undertaking too many objectives—or by the decision to undertake *no* objectives because they cannot reach unity.

A second observation offers encouragement and warning: corporate creativity can lead a group toward unconventional methods! And, perhaps it should. Once-powerful practices can become dull routines with time. Worn-out habits silently entrench themselves, catching groups unaware. In the case of Riverside, the fact that these initiatives emerge from waiting on the Holy Spirit and from a corporate process ensures that the decisions are appropriate to this congregation. The same cannot always be said of individual-driven creativity that is imposed on a group, or of corporate decisions that have not been shaped by the Spirit.

Creativity will invariably lead a group into uncharted territory. Such change can induce anxiety among the participants. Not every new initiative will succeed. Even groups supportive of change will often find themselves surprisingly resistant to new ideas. Thus, new initiatives such as these demand courage and patience.

One appealing theme in the Riverside story is the church's ability to overcome programmed Friends' allergy to evangelism. From this church, we learn two compelling features that must be given attention by meetings. First, the group must grow beyond defining evangelism or outreach in negative terms. It is not sufficient to say "Friends don't do . . ." as an answer to Friends' position on outreach. Vital meetings will, instead, determine they will offer the gift of their faith to their community. Second, they must articulate the means by which they will share this gift.

At some point, a group must ask how far it is willing to venture from the traditional norms and practices of its family. Worship styles and outreach methods vary from location to location among Friends, making it impossible to say with absolute clarity what "Friends do" or "Friends don't do." It is important for Friends to ask how they maintain connection with their heritage even as they devise innovative ways to practice their faith with personal integrity.

Riverside Friends Church
Founded: 1979
Affiliation(s): Iowa Yearly Meeting
                  Friends United Meeting

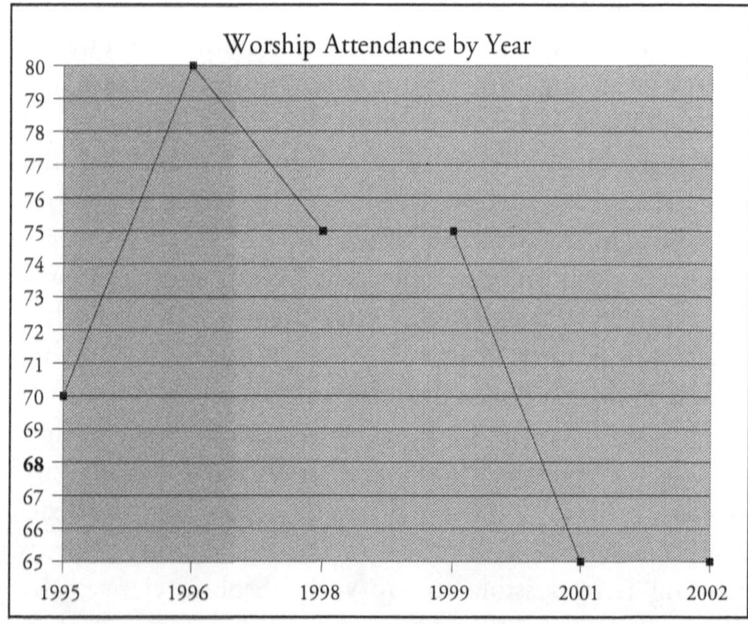

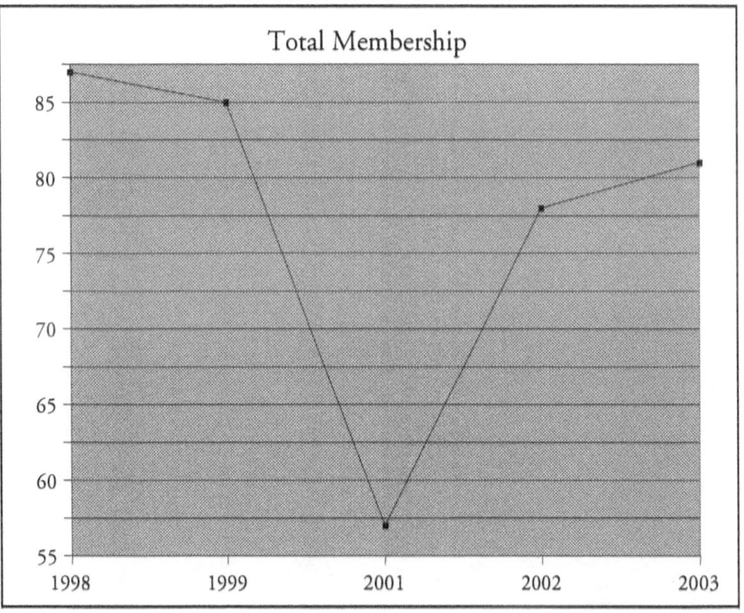
Total Membership
85
80
75
70
65
60
55
1998
1999
2001
2002
2003

Sing Sing Worship Group
354 Hunter Street, Ossining, NY 10562
New York Yearly Meeting (FGC/FUM)

Established: 1987   **Attendance: 40**

"Give me something to believe in . . ."

Many Americans dream of a home on a river. A group of
Friends in New York have one, though they would all
prefer a change of address. This home is not a version of
the American dream, complete with images of a peaceful,
idyllic existence. There are no leisurely afternoons spent
on a wrap-around front porch, secure in the gentle
motion of a favorite rocking chair while sipping a tall
glass of iced tea. The house is not bordered by a well-
kept lawn. The joy of children's laughter does not echo
against the sound of the river's constant movement.
Instead, this home houses a great collection of heartbreak
and tragedy created from poor choices and broken
dreams.

A tall fence topped with barbed wire replaces the
well-kept garden and lawn. This home on the river is
filled with sounds, but listen closely before you respond
or react, for every sound requires an extra moment for
interpretation. Plenty is spent on home security, with
uniformed officers and even bars over all possible exits.

This place, which some Friends call home, is
located on a river–the Hudson River, to be specific. The
view is indeed magnificent, creating the type of ambiance
in which a good, slow cup of coffee would be a
wonderful way to start a morning if only the bars over

the windows did not spoil the view. This house on the river is literally the "big house." The phrase "sent up the river" was coined with this place in mind. This "house" is Sing Sing prison. Behind its thick walls and iron bars a small but powerful Quaker worship group exists. It is both a seed of faith inside the joint and a testimony to the transforming power of God through the Quaker witness.

One might wonder how a Quaker worship group begins in prison. Such groups may be established when an inmate requests one. If there are Friends on the outside who are willing to travel to the prison for worship, a group is then easily formed. Visitors sign in with the warden rather than on pew pads. An usher, who is armed with a weapon rather than a bulletin, escorts visitors to their seats. But other than passing through a metal detector and needing a bit more time than usual to reach the designated worship room, there are more similarities than differences between a local meeting and this worship group. One discovers approximately thirty-five to forty men choose to participate in the Quaker worship group at Sing Sing prison. This accounts for about two percent of the prison population.

In many cases, Quaker involvement with prison ministry originates in the Alternatives to Violence (AVP) project. AVP was formed in 1975 as the result of a collaborative project between Quakers and inmates of Greenhaven Prison. Workshops offered to prisoners focus upon recidivism reduction, coping with prison violence, and re-introduction to society. AVP workshops have been an integral part of the Quaker witness at Sing Sing.

At least four area Friends regularly worship with the Sing Sing Quaker Worship Group. Besides their interest in AVP, parts of their own personal journey convince them this is where they should be present during worship on a given Sunday. One Friend recognizes his own sense of being a wounded healer. With that self-recognition, his participation with the worship group is an important part of his ministry. A Friend who is a poet and dancer at heart is a strong advocate for AVP and dedicated to group work. A third Friend has experienced a redefinition of love as the heart of the universe as a result of his role as a grandfather. Another recognizes the distinction between "church" and "ministry" and wants to commend and support the worship group for exercising genuine ministry. Together with inmates who choose to do so, these Friends participate in a vital ministry within the confines of Sing Sing.

Visible Vitality
Worship

The room where these Friends worship is pleasant, but bare. It is a setting in which Quaker's rejection of symbols works well! As inmates enter the room, the air is abuzz with the sound of the fellowship of reconnecting. Light refreshments are available, more important for the brief feeling of autonomy they grant than for their taste or nutritional value.

As worship begins, the group sits in a circle, as do many unprogrammed meetings. That hour of silence is more than an hour of worship. It is an hour of freedom! As one Friend expressed, "In the silence I am free to be without worry that someone will tell me where to go or what to do. For that period of time, I feel liberated." Indeed, this worship group provides moments of liberation in important ways. In a system that is prone to depersonalize, this is a group that restores identity. These are more than prisoners serving sentences; these are men with hurts, hopes and dreams. Here are a few of those dreams, with no names attached for the sake of those who may not wish their identities revealed.

> "I am a writer who has yet to write. The act of writing reinvents me. The Bible helps me to recognize myself and inspires me. The call of Matthew teaches that everybody deserves a second chance."

> "I am a native of New York. I once sought to be a help to others. Now I'm working on self-improvement and marketing myself. I have been here for thirteen years. I was raised as a Jehovah's Witness, but rejected that faith. I am now on a spiritual path seeking something to believe in."

> "I am a child of God. God dwells within. I am a spiritual being having a human experience. I have been forgiven a tremendous amount . . . a lot is required of me."

> "I am a Christian who worships with Quakers. I used to point at others as the

cause of my problems. I now see that I am the cause. I have experienced real repentance. I would like the chance to be the man I could be."

The self-disclosure contained in these statements is admirable, and an indication of the rich community experienced within the safe confines of the Sing Sing worship group. In prison, one never wants to be exposed or appear vulnerable. Alternate identities are the rule rather than the exception. Residents adopt nicknames by which to be known. Against that backdrop, this worship group creates a sacred space within the larger system. It is a place where participants experience respect. It is a group which reclaims dignity for one another. It is a community that reframes identity, ushering in the type of newness of life that the Bible describes and for which believers should long.

Perhaps the greatest gift that occurs within the Quaker worship group is the momentary freedom it provides to those who attend. Prison life is highly structured. Basic elements of life such as movement from one place to another, the range of activities in which one participates, where and when one enjoys recreation, even when one eats or showers, are highly restricted. A higher human authority constantly sets the agenda and dictates the routine. These periods of worship provide a brief respite from the highly structured life of prison. In worship, one has the option to be still and silent. There among other fellow travelers in the Body of Christ, labels and barriers are set aside–"there is neither male nor female, Greek nor Jew" the apostle Paul wrote.

Ministry

The word "ministry" is closely connected with faith communities and righteous living, neither of which immediately comes to mind when one thinks of life behind bars. After all, prisons are populated with people who have broken the law–something that is seldom associated with righteous behavior unless the topic is civil disobedience. When the term "ministry" *is* associated with prison life, the usual reference is to an outside group bringing the Good News to those who are imprisoned. Seldom, however, does one expect to encounter ministers residing behind bars.

Members of the Quaker Worship Group at Sing Sing challenge all of those stereotypes. For those who are able to accept a working definition of ministry as simply "service"—which is at the heart of the Greek word from which the term "ministry" is derived—it is easy to identify ministry of an extremely high caliber among these inmates. It occurs without any further trappings of office, ritual, or dogma. These Friends do not discuss the *concept* of ministry. Rather, they give their attention to the *care* of other members in the group.

There are visible, unofficial leaders within this group. However, ministry in this setting is largely a shared responsibility expressed in the performance of various chores throughout the prison community. These chores include teaching, mentoring, and actions of human service. These men provide core leadership in several service groups, including: Prisoners for Aids Counseling Service (PACE); Hudson Link (Non-Profit advocates for prison education); Certificate in Ministry Program; Rehabilitation through the Arts (RTA);

Alternatives to Violence Program (AVP); Youth Intervention Program (YIP); Youth Assistance Program (YAP); Aggression Replacement Training (ART); and Alcohol & Substance Abuse Treatment (ASAT).

In this setting, discovery of spiritual gifts and calls to ministry is primarily an informal process that occurs through encouragement to explore and experience revelation. When members of the group discover possible calls to ministry, the group encourages enrollment in the locally sponsored Certificate in Ministry program or the Masters in Professional Studies. Because of this unusual setting, members of the group have more time to devote to study. A high percentage of the group has been involved in formal study of theology and ministry. Though unsuccessful, the group has attempted to secure funding for additional masters-level theological education through correspondence.

Community

Community shared by the members of this worship group is one of the strongest features of their vitality. It is nothing short of a counter-cultural environment. Within a system that minimizes and dehumanizes, the worship group establishes a place where dignity, respect, and even new identity is found.

The men at Sing Sing live with some important paradoxes. First, they live in an environment that is paradoxically controlled, but uncontrolled. Movement and activity are severely restricted. Someone else determines where a person resides and when that person may leave their room. The "neighborhood" is populated, yet no one there chose this particular cast of characters as their most immediate neighbors–an important fact to acknowledge, given that many persons choose their neighborhoods based on available amenities and support systems. Particularly in the act of choosing where to worship, personal comfort and the ability to develop meaningful connections with the community are of prime importance.

Recognizing this reality, the second half of the paradox becomes apparent. The individual has no real influence over who is their neighbor or the type of associations and activities that operate beneath the official power structures. It is there, beneath the official structures, that different social structures rule relationships. Those are frequently based on fear and intimidation. They depend upon strength to subordinate or avoid one's enemies. Loyalty is rewarded; alternatives are not pretty. The motives and values that drive this underground society are almost always at odds with the values of a faith community. Challenging those deeply ingrained structures is difficult, even perilous. Yet, a religious community influenced by Quaker faith cannot help but make those challenges.

Residents of Sing Sing live with another paradox as well. These men have ample time for study, reflection and conversation. These are the large blocks of uninterrupted time of which persons working sixty hour weeks can only dream. Without sufficient resources and motivation, this luxury of time amounts to squandered potential. Unfortunately, mentors and educational opportunities are scarce. Even if a person utilizes every opportunity for education, growth, and personal transformation, there is paradoxically little tangible advantage to these outcomes within the prison setting. These improvements will only be a significant advantage in the event of release from prison.

With these identified paradoxes, the Sing Sing worship group has succeeded, at the most foundational level, of creating a counter-cultural community. Participants in this group enjoy a genuine community founded upon faith and grounded in Christian love and respect. It is further shaped by an amazing hospitality that pervades the association these men have with each other. They greet one another with respect, frequently choosing to use their given names with one another rather than the nickname by which they are called in the larger prison population. Names like Coco, Whoa-Whoa, Knowledge, and Papa Smurf are set aside. For a few brief moments, the names of their birth were brought out of the closet, dusted off, and worn with pride.

Fellowship surrounding refreshments—fruit juice and pastries—provides extended moments of communion. Smiles are abundant. Spiritual energy charges the atmosphere. Emotions of release, relief, and expectation all contribute to the joy of the moment, preparing hearts and minds for a period of expectant, waiting, worship.

Invisible Supports
Spiritual Foundations

This worship group includes persons from various cultures, both ethnically and religiously. Their paths of spiritual formation defy categorization. Prior Roman Catholic and Protestant associations are amply represented, as are Buddhist affiliations. Many participants were reared in families without committed religious affiliations. On more than one occasion, the life story of these persons reveals that Sing Sing or other detention facilities have been their "home" for most of their life. One participant who has spent most of his life in one prison or another said, "I came to this country in 1959. I have never really known what it means to be free." Consequently a common theological language is unlikely to develop naturally.

Within this worship group, the most common shared belief is founded upon the idea of one God whose spirit indwells all humankind. While general in many ways, it is perfect for this setting. It is free of required rituals or ordained personnel that are inaccessible to this group. It transcends denominational bias and baggage that may exist from earlier experiences. It acknowledges a higher power *and* includes them all within the chosen group. Building upon the general description, this shared belief is conducive to an understanding of God that is highly experiential and not bound to specific times or places. Experiencing God in silence is a core theological tenet, grounding their practice of worship. In that setting, basic human equality in the eyes of God occurs in theory and in practice. Particular theological details receive less emphasis from the group than "right living" and a commitment to non-violence.

Community Life

It would be inaccurate to state that community does not exist in prison anywhere except the worship group. However, the worship group is a decidedly different type of community than the surrounding population. The question becomes, then, how does this community relate to the larger population?

The understanding of ministry as "service" is once again operative. The community offers an open "quarterly meeting" as an entrance point for other prisoners to explore the group and determine whether or not they wish to participate on a regular basis. It also provides a photocopying service to inmates who are litigating their criminal appeals or parole violations. In this manner, the community offers a form of service or outreach to the wider population.

Lessons on Vitality

Many meetings struggle with their sense of identity and purpose. Long past those early years when enthusiastic fires burned bright in pioneering charter members, many meetings and churches look remarkably like the status quo of their immediate community. In such cases, the faith practices there no longer appear to be an alternative that beckons us to embrace a higher cause. It becomes, instead, a competitor for our allegiance, time, and money. The most powerful vitality lesson from the Sing Sing worship group relates to their role as a counter-cultural movement. Meetings seeking revitalization should ask themselves what it will take to reclaim a sense of radical witness that challenges unjust and violent power structures that support the status quo. They will want to discern how they can offer an alternative of meaningful interactions that are grounded in their spiritual foundation and transformative for their neighborhood.

Sing Sing also offers useful insights on the power of identity within the faith community. Despite the lack of developed theological language and religious ritual, powerful personal transformation occurs within this community that understands that hospitality and respect are closely associated with Divine love. Any meeting or church that aspires to be a vital community will want to consider how hospitality and respect help minister to broken lives and how their ministry contributes to a transformative faith identity.

Finally, simple acts of support can be fundamental to healthy, vital meetings. Not every idea, project, or new ministry must be grandiose, elaborate or costly. Simple gestures that demonstrate support and concern can be great catalysts in a meeting or church's renewal. As groups assist others in their efforts to grow and improve, the group receives a reciprocal benefit from the change.

Sing Sing Worship Group
Founded: 1986
Affiliation(s): Purchase Quarterly Meeting
        New York Yearly Meeting
        Friends General Conference
        Friends United Meeting

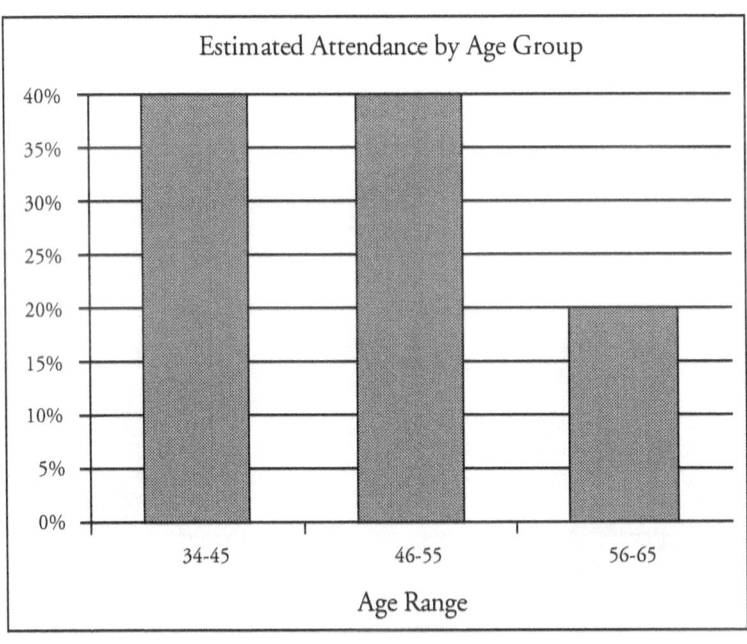

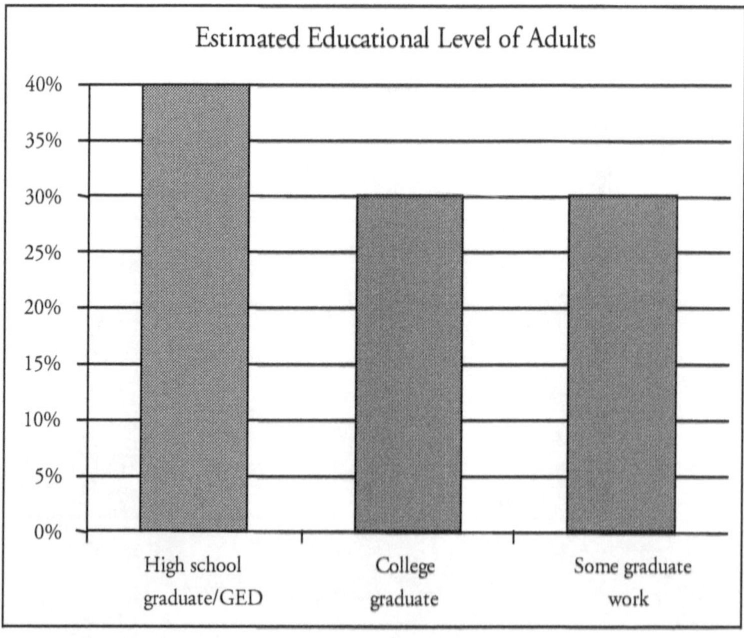

Estimated Educational Level of Adults
40%
35%
30%
25%
20%
15%
10%
5%
0%
High school
graduate/GED
College
graduate
Some graduate
work

West Richmond Friends Meeting
609 West Main Street, Richmond, Indiana 47374
Indiana Yearly Meeting (FUM)

Established: 1909   Membership: 147

"I do not call you servants any longer . . . but I have called you Friends . . ." (John 15:15)

The splintering of Friends groups over time has created sister groups that are starkly different from one another. The variations are well known. Programmed groups utilize the office of pastor as an integral part of their ministry and tend to be more Christocentric; their unprogrammed counterparts choose not to utilize the services of designated pastoral leaders and are usually more universalistic in their theology. The West Richmond Meeting blends the richest components of these two Quaker branches. They release a Friend for pastoral ministry but maintain a strong commitment to universal ministry. They uphold a strong commitment to Christ but define the parameters of Christianity much more broadly than many of its programmed peers. In a religious tradition that often describes itself in polar terms, West Richmond Friends Meeting exemplifies a blended version of the Friends faith that attempts to reconcile the Quaker tradition with itself.

In 1909, three Quaker congregations located on the eastern side of Richmond agreed to establish a Friends meeting on the western side of the city. West Richmond meeting was born as a result of this decision. From the beginning, its proximity to Earlham College influenced the character of this meeting. The first pastors, Elbert Russell and Murray Kenworthy, were professors of Biblical Literature at the college.

Almost one hundred years later, several Earlham faculty and staff members will be seen in worship on any given Sunday, but the meeting draws from a much wider area than the college campus. West Richmond members have varied religious backgrounds and faith journeys. The meeting's intergenerational flair and its involvement of children in the life of the meeting has served as a strong attraction for several decades. Some Friends cite its commitment to the social gospel and community service—emphases that can be traced back at least to the 1920s—especially as a means of incorporating the Quaker witness and the biblical faith as the meeting's most appealing quality. The usual influences of family connections and relocation to the Richmond area contribute to the steady stream of new arrivals at the meeting. Some suggest that the kind of people who hate organized religion are among those who love West Richmond the most, as this meeting has a holistic, organic dynamic that manages to avoid the stodginess of typical "church life."

Visible Vitality
Worship

Though arriving Friends joyfully greet one another upon entering the meetinghouse, worship begins quietly at West Richmond Meeting. Friends take their seats and begin to center themselves in preparation for and anticipation of worship. Though seemingly casual and informal, and certainly open to being redirected by the Holy Spirit, meeting for worship is thoughtfully planned by a small committee that bears responsibility for prayerfully developing and coordinating meeting for worship.

A typical Sunday morning service includes warm welcomes, and readings appropriate to the occasion. It offers wonderfully sung music, some by the congregation and some by the choir. A children's moment invites young Friends to the front of the room for a story or brief message. A sermon, typically fifteen minutes in length, contributes to the worship experience. Following the sermon, meeting members enter deep silence, worshiping and waiting with expectation. Friends frequently speak from the silence. At the conclusion of worship, the meeting ends with a handshake.

Some use the term "semi-programmed worship" to describe this style of meeting for worship. It includes the usual elements of a programmed worship service, but with a few noteworthy characteristics. First, the entire service is seasoned with silence. Nothing moves quickly as the group progresses through worship together. Second, unlike many Protestant and programmed Friends meetings, the sermon is not seen as the apex of the worship as though it is the ultimate moment during which God speaks to the people. Instead, the elements of the programmed worship prepare persons for and lead them to a climactic communion with God in the silence. In this sense, this format unites the best of two forms of worship within the body of Friends.

Ministry

The West Richmond Meeting embraces the long-standing Friends belief in universal ministry practiced by its members. This understanding of ministry not only describes their belief that all persons are gifted for some form of ministry; it also shapes the manner in which the meeting defines the role of the pastoral minister. In this setting, the understanding that the pastor is merely one minister among ministers is much more than rhetoric used to limit the authority of the pastor. Instead, it defines the larger responsibility of the members of the meeting and their joint responsibility for the care and nurture of the meeting.

As West Richmond employs a pastoral minister, it does so with a clear intention toward a team ministry approach. This team approach was one decision made as a result of a year of pastoral transition during which the meeting utilized the services of an interim minister and a consultative process. The team approach was utilized by the meeting at an earlier period, but ended when the team leader left the meeting. Given the ideals and commitments of the meeting, as well as its unusually high ratio of skilled, capable leaders, this model of ministry works well in this setting.

As examples of the practical implications of this ministry strategy, a committee that includes the pastor has responsibility for planning worship throughout the year. They give prayerful thought to the needs of the meeting and the issues facing persons of faith, then map out the expected foci of worship in the months ahead. The meeting also expects that the pastor will be responsible for delivering the Sunday-morning sermon only two or three times each month. On the remaining Sundays, members of the meeting or guest speakers are invited to preach. Rather than undermining the pastor, the meeting sees this practice as an opportunity to lessen the potential burden of pastoral ministry and cultivate the gifts others have to provide leadership in worship.

Discovering gifts for ministry is a fairly high priority at West Richmond, although there is no official or standard corporate process through which this occurs. This is one setting where the very ethos of the spiritual community contributes to the facilitation of gift discovery. The pastor and Ministry and Oversight Committee assist this process, but an even greater factor is the manner in which individuals encourage one another. The meeting frequently utilizes clearness committees to support persons who are exploring potential calls to ministry. Sometimes, all involved are surprised by what emerges, as when a couple in the meeting recently discovered a call to work in foreign mission work.

Another significant component of ministry at West Richmond is evident in their commitment to religious education. Friends here do not want the usual, generic brand of Sunday School curriculum. Because the meeting understands its principal gift as empowering members to care for one another in multiple ways, including spiritual sharing and mutual support, the educational ministry is designed to support this principal gift. With the many qualified persons in the meeting— Earlham faculty, retired pastors and missionaries, leaders in affiliated religious organizations—West Richmond has an ample supply of capable and creative teachers. Over half of the meeting is involved in the Sunday School program. Approximately ten percent of the budget goes to educational ministry. Nearly thirty percent of the labor involved comes from volunteer hours.

Outreach

A strong orientation toward service pervades West Richmond's posture toward community outreach. As it serves, the meeting emphasizes a strong Quaker witness in the community. Their presence is evident in multiple ways. Many members are active in local organizations within the community and understand their volunteer support as a means of sharing Quaker support in the community. Approximately ten percent of their members are appointed to boards and committees of affiliated Friends organizations, demonstrating their understanding of the importance of being connected to the larger body of Friends and their commitment to strengthening it. Quaker organizations that benefit from West Richmond members' time and leadership include:

- American Friends Service Committee
- Associated Committee of Friends on Indian Affairs
- Earlham College
- Earlham School of Religion
- Friends Association for Higher Education
- Friends Committee on National Legislation
- Friends Council on Education
- Friends Fellowship Community
- Friends United Meeting

- Friends World Committee for Consultation
- Indiana Yearly Meeting
- Quaker Hill Conference Center
- Richmond Quarterly Meeting
- Richmond Young Friends
- United Society of Friends Women

Even as West Richmond members directly serve certain groups and organizations, the meeting serves as a hospitable host for several other groups. The following groups use or have used space at the meetinghouse for offices or regular meetings:

- On Earth Peace – a ministry that provides assistance to congregations that want to increase their peace ministry

- Emergency Material Aids Program of the American Friends Service Committee – an office at West Richmond Friends collects used clothing, friendship kits and other practical materials for shipment around the world

- Friends World Committee for Consultation (FWCC) – the Midwest office is located at West Richmond Friends

- Alcoholics Anonymous – meets regularly at the meetinghouse

- Narcotics Anonymous – meets regularly at the meetinghouse

- Boy Scouts – meets regularly at the meetinghouse

- Adult School – a current events and literature discussion group meets during the school year

- Birth to Five – a play group and parent support for pre-school children

- La Leche League – a support and training group for nursing mothers

Other local causes that benefit regularly from West Richmond's interest, including appointments to their boards and committees include:

- AIDS Task Force of Richmond
- Community Food Pantry
- CROP Walk
- Habitat for Humanity
- ICHTHYS House
- Interfaith Apartments

Invisible Supports
Spiritual Foundations

West Richmond Meeting is unapologetically Christian with an equal commitment to remaining nondogmatic. As noted earlier, some suggest that people love coming to West Richmond because they hate organized religion. Containing a healthy mix of individuals who choose such labels as evangelical, liberal, and civic Christian, Friends here are able to describe themselves as disciples of Christ, yet welcome seekers who may not be able to claim the disciple identity for themselves.

Given the diversity of viewpoints present among members, Friends at West Richmond are more united by practices than a particular set of beliefs. In this setting, Friends believe that Christianity is about living and means to "include" not "exclude." Faith is understood as "trust in God" rather than "belief in God." Conversation together can be the context in which the Holy Spirit works. For that reason, the meeting creates ample time and space for such work to occur. "Joining with the meeting" means not that a person has arrived at their final stage of spiritual maturity, but that they are in a process with others at the meeting all of whom seek to grow in their understanding and practice of faithful living.

The Bible, Quaker testimonies, and the leading of the Spirit are frequently referenced as important resources for guidance and direction. However, the emphasis on practice and process creates a setting in which shared beliefs will be broad ones in spite of those shared resources. In general, conversations about common theology gravitate toward language that describes God's love and care for ***all*** people. Prayer and meditation are key means by which this loving God communicates care and directs the lives of seekers. In particular, this direction offers guidance on how it is that Friends do God's work on earth, both individually and corporately.

Vision and Business Processes

Business of the meeting is conducted in monthly meeting sessions. Open to the entire meeting, only twenty to thirty members attend regularly. The meeting also relies upon a healthy system of functioning committees to facilitate various ministries and projects. Throughout the meeting structure, the meeting relies on good clerking skills to help the group discern the sense of the meeting in accord with good Quaker process.

West Richmond does not have a formally adopted mission statement or an overarching vision toward which they are working. Conversation with members suggests a common purpose that seeks to praise God and bless each other while presenting a Quaker presence and witness to the community. In any event, the lack of a formal statement or vision does not appear to be detrimental due to their commitment to conversation, process, and leadership by the body. For example, during their pastor's sabbatical, the meeting used this period to engage a consultant with a goal of gaining a snapshot of their meeting's status and aspirations. Though no concrete vision or strategy emerged, the results of that brief study continues to fuel conversation about the meeting's future projects and direction.

Their life together demonstrates a commitment to experience God and seek the knowledge of Christ, to share in ministry and leadership, and to serve one another and the community. As an example, when Friends gather for worship at West Richmond, they are doing more than just attending worship. They are contributing to and participating in the work of God. To that end, they have high expectations of quality, authenticity and integrity. The implications of these expectations are in evidence in a set of Bill of Rights posted on the meeting's website. The list is the result of an Adult Forum class discussion about a set of minimum standards members and attendees have a right to expect. These include;

- You have the right to take part in worship.
- You have the right to be safe in our meeting.
- You have the right to take part in decisions made by the meeting.
- You have the right to know where money which you have given is being used.
- You have the right not to be asked for money improperly
- You have the right to see all public documents of the meeting.
- You have the right to privacy.

- You have the right to the services of the meeting.
- You have the right to worship with integrity.
- You have the right to the support and discipline of the meeting.

West Richmond displays an admirable tendency to be in frequent conversation about what it means to be a person of faith and how such persons work together in the context of a faith community. The conversations provide cause for self-examination and give rise to creative initiatives that serve God, the meeting, and the community.

Lessons on Vitality

The Religious Society of Friends bears the scars of its numerous schisms. One debilitating effect of those schisms is a high level of suspicion of "the other Friends." Another effect is the rigid separation of spiritual practices into "programmed" and "unprogrammed" means of worship. One of the most powerful contributions to the quest for vitality offered by West Richmond is their commitment to embrace the strengths of both styles of worship. They demonstrate that good sermons can make an important contribution to worship, but not at the expense of listening to the Spirit in silence. They illustrate the value of long periods of silence, but without sacrificing the contribution of the prepared spoken word.

West Richmond also provides a wonderful example of "universal ministry" powerfully lived. They recognize the need for a pastoral minister in their setting, but are equally clear as to the appropriate role for that minister. Meanwhile, capable members offer leadership as clerks, committee members, teachers, and more. Such a system can work when the meeting appreciates and defines the role of the pastor and when the pastor is able to celebrate shared ministry and leadership.

For those Friends who shy away from mission statements or formal vision plans for a variety of reasons, West Richmond illustrates a healthy alternative. In a word, it is "conversation." This is a meeting that is willing to engage almost any issue, whether it be offering a committee for clearness to Friends who are seeking answers, or wrestling with the justice implications surrounding same-sex unions. Their willingness to talk openly and at deep levels about such a wide range of issues keeps them from resting on past laurels or sitting idly by while the world bleeds to death.

West Richmond Monthly Meeting
Founded: 1909
Affiliation(s): Indiana Yearly Meeting
                Friends United Meeting

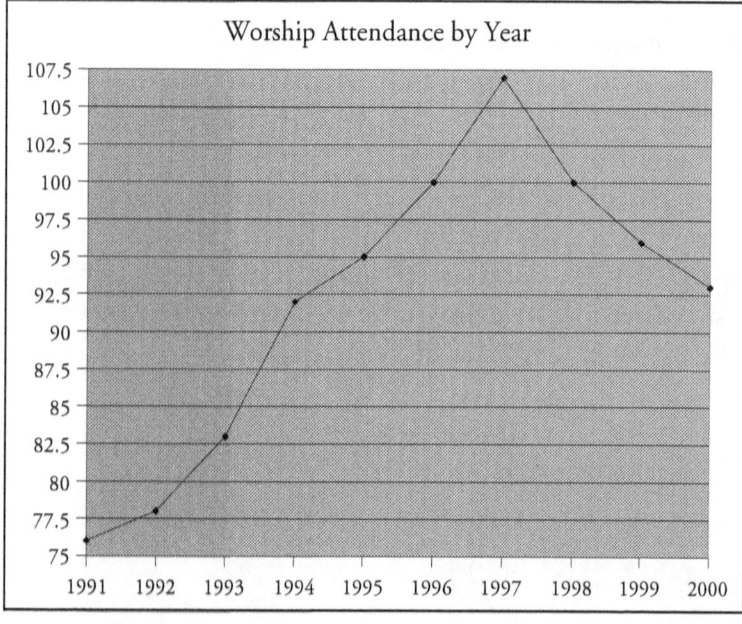

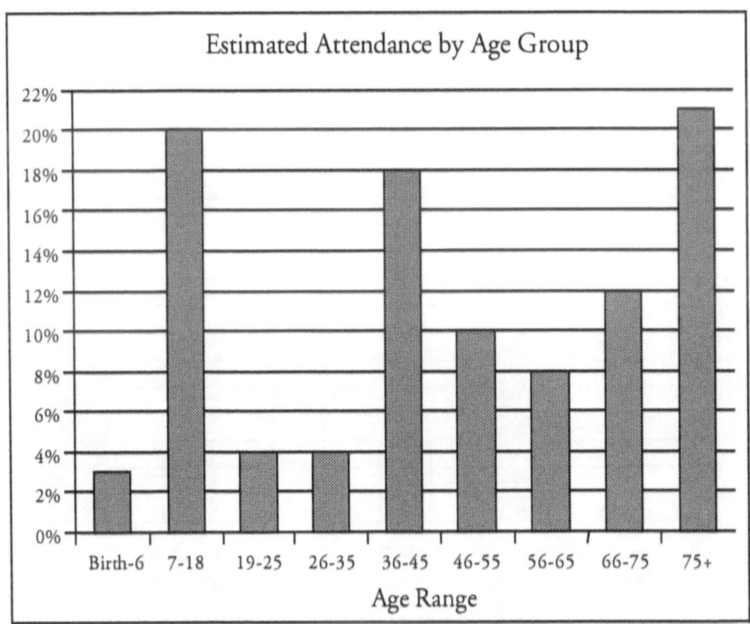
Estimated Attendance by Age Group
22%
20%
18%
16%
14%
12%
10%
8%
6%
4%
2%
0%
Birth-6
7-18
19-25
26-35
36-45
46-55
56-65
66-75
75+
Age Range

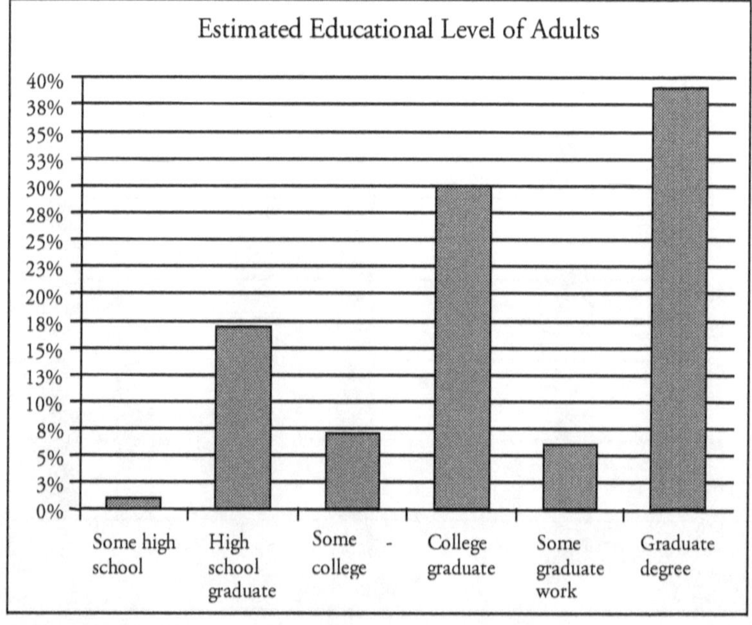

Estimated Educational Level of Adults
40%
38%
35%
33%
30%
28%
25%
23%
20%
18%
15%
13%
10%
8%
5%
3%
0%
Some high school
High school graduate
Some college
College graduate
Some graduate work
Graduate degree

Westfield Friends Meeting
324 South Union Street, Westfield, IN 46074
Western Yearly Meeting (FUM)

Established: 1835   Membership: 240

"For where two or three are gathering in my name, I am there among them." (Matthew 18:20)

A great conversion is underway. Much of rural Indiana is being transformed from its quiet agrarian roots to a highly populated, bustling suburban community. New traffic patterns, fresh business opportunities, and pressing municipal needs are only part of the changing picture. With the influx of new families, social dynamics are reshaped. Indeed, the communal ethos of the neighborhood changes. In the midst of these developments, churches and meetings face the overwhelming question of how to fulfill their mission. Those who opt for a "head in the sand" approach will, intentionally or otherwise, portray an isolationist or even oppositional mentality that is reclusive. Congregations who embrace the changes as new ministry opportunities will possibly contribute to the spiritual foundation and formation of the evolving community. In recent years, Westfield Friends Meeting has faced this very scenario.

Westfield is located north of Indianapolis, Indiana and is making the transition from a rural, agricultural community to a suburban, business community. The population of the town has tripled in the last ten years. Historically an almost exclusively Caucasian community, that demographic is beginning to change as well. As a result, neither size, composition, nor cultural norm of this pleasant town are what they were a decade ago.

In the midst of such rapid growth, Westfield Friends Meeting is experiencing a surge of its own. From 1996-2002 the meeting experienced a fifty-four percent growth in worship attendance, increasing from an average of 124 in 1996 to 191 in 2002. Somewhat surprisingly, as the town of Westfield experiences a rapid increase of new families, much of Westfield Friends' growth is coming from people with long-term roots in the community. Among the members of the meeting, one finds persons who are descended from the first white settlers of the area. Another family is the fourth generation to attend Westfield meeting. Some are Friends new to the area, who have re-located here due to employment. Still others, with a variety of Christian and non-Christian backgrounds, are new to Friends. They have been attracted by some facet of worship and ministry in the meeting.

The meetinghouse has the appearance of a fairly traditional church with white exterior and a modest steeple. However, since 1994 the meeting has invested over $750,000 in its property during two different renovation projects. In many ways, this is a reflection of the meeting's approach to ministry. With a strong commitment to its Quaker heritage, it also keeps abreast of contemporary trends in worship—"innovation rooted in the Friends' tradition," as one member describes it. Traditional Christian beliefs and practices dominate the vision and practice of the meeting; however, some of the most significant experiences occur in newer ministries that combine discipleship with relational connections.

Visible Vitality
Worship

Worship at Westfield Friends contains the traditional components of programmed worship in the manner of Friends. Biblical preaching from a Quaker perspective is a core component of the experience, as is open worship. The services feature a variety of musical contributions. These, along with the Spirit of the Lord and the warmth of the people create an inviting opportunity for worship.

When Friends at Westfield speak about their worship experience, the usual components cited above are mentioned and appreciated. However, the conversation quickly gravitates elsewhere. Two descriptions loom large in their discussions. First, worship is not limited to a Sunday morning experience. Many are involved in small groups throughout the year. These groups, ranging from formal Bible study to exercise groups to informal gatherings, are an oasis for building spiritual friendships that provide support and encouragement to its participants. They provide social anchors into the network of relationships there. Second, members of the meeting describe worship as a healing experience. By this, some refer to a healing of the soul, as personal wounds are made whole. Others describe emotional and spiritual healing as their lives are transformed by Christ. At least one physical healing is cited, when after prayer a pending surgery was canceled when physicians could no longer find traces of cancer.

An important common thread that weaves through the descriptions of various healings is the role of personal relationships. Without doubt, their relationship with Christ is primary, but their personal relationships with one another are integral to this vital experience. In the words of one Friend, "the sincerity of relationships with one another makes maintaining the mask difficult."

Ministry

Westfield is a programmed meeting. It employs a pastor and an associate pastor, and receives quality ministry and leadership from each position. However, the Quaker understanding of a universal call to ministry remains strong at the meeting—a fact that has several practical implications.

One implication is the style of leadership the meeting utilizes. Though they are accustomed to strong pastoral leaders, the preferred style of leadership is consultative from leaders who are willing to be vulnerable. Leadership by example rather than by territory thrives at Westfield, as achieved influence wins respect. And, leadership is not limited to the the pastoral staff. As the church cultivates ministry among all people, it also calls forth leadership for all age groups and in a variety of capacities. In describing what leaders look like at Westfield, the list was brief, but revealing:

- Walks with Christ
- Has a quiet presence
- Earns respect
- Not limited to a particular age bracket
- Lifestyle supports their words

A second implication is the meeting's focus on assisting all believers in understanding their call and gifts for ministry. In recent years, workshops on spiritual gifts by the pastor and yearly meeting superintendent have been supplemented by Ministry and Counsel's commitment to make this emphasis a regular component of their care for the meeting. Even with this corporate commitment to help members discern their gifts and calls to ministry, the group insists that individual leadings are more important than institutional efforts.

Finally, all ministry at Westfield has spiritual transformation as its goal. Their highest priority is to introduce persons to Christ, understanding that ultimately only God can do the necessary work within the hearts of the people. Even as these Friends have an expectation that discipleship leads to conformity with Christ, they are able to acknowledge that everyone has their own process for spiritual growth. No matter where a person happens to be on his or her journey, they are loved.

Small Groups

The journey of faith is always personal and experiential. At Westfield, small groups deepen and strengthen the bonds formed in the larger, corporate worship. Traditional age-defined Sunday School classes are available for youth and children, as are two youth groups. A Wednesday evening prayer group, United Society of Friends Women, and Quaker Men also meet regularly. In addition, many members participate in Adult Growth Groups, designed to provide small group settings for learning and fellowship. A Women's

Ministry group meets monthly, providing a connecting point for the meeting's female population. Monthly fellowship, speakers, and Bible study, as well as an annual retreat, nurture community among the women of the meeting. Sports teams participate in local church leagues. Family Fun Nights and the annual Vacation Bible School round out a full slate of educational and social activities that contribute to the formation and socialization at Westfield meeting as members are together on many occasions outside of Sunday morning worship.

These groups make an important contribution to the vitality of Westfield Meeting. They are a source through which faith is nourished and nurtured in the lives of participating members. They also support efforts to identify and cultivate leadership within the meeting. And, they provide an easy way to integrate new attenders into the wider body of the meeting and give them a sense of personal belonging.

The meeting's demographic composition is interesting to consider at this point. Thirty-five percent of the meeting is age eighteen or younger. Another twenty-six percent is between ages thirty-five and fifty-five. Only sixteen percent is older than sixty-five years of age. It would be inaccurate to suggest that all age groups do not need social contacts. However, parents typically want their children involved in activities outside of the home, and many parents themselves seek support from their peers. These tendencies may provide a clue to the popularity and vitality of small groups at Westfield.

Invisible Supports
Spiritual Foundations

For Westfield Friends, the central, most uniting, theological belief is simple: Jesus Christ is the Son of God and through him alone individuals may attain salvation. The meeting describes itself as "Christ-centered without embarrassment," and places great emphasis upon an individual's salvation experience and personal relationship with Christ.

The authority of the Bible is also embraced without reservation among Friends here. This is evident both in their affirmation that the Bible is authoritative **and** in the fact that the Bible itself is the authoritative source used to legitimate many other statements of belief. Beliefs about God, Jesus, sin, morality, and more, are true because they are drawn from the biblical witness.

An understanding of human sinfulness and redemptive grace ranks among the highest common theological bonds within the meeting. Friends here possess an approach to faith that acknowledges the ravages of sin but looks for transformation and healing in the lives of believers. Faith, therefore, involves belief, action and accountability—a biblical position that Westfield Friends associate with George Fox's view on a believer's perfection in Christ.

The meeting also places high value on Western Yearly Meeting's *Faith and Practice* as a document of weighty authority. One of the strongest Quaker influences on the belief system of Westfield Friends relates to their views on the Holy Spirit. Friends' long-standing belief in the presence of the Inner Light leads to recognition of the value of discernment. This theological tenet affects ministry, worship, and decision-making. As noted earlier, Westfield Friends describe ministry as the responsibility of all its members and give institutional support to discerning calls to and gifts for ministry. In worship, these Friends wait upon the Holy Spirit and seek to be ministered to by the Spirit through spiritual communion. On occasion, the movement of the Spirit is such that the pastor chooses not to deliver a sermon. The practice of discernment also supports their business process, where prayerful deliberation leads to a sense of the meeting.

Vision and Business Processes

The Westfield Friends Meeting seems to have succeeded where many other businesses and groups fail—they have a mission statement **and** their members know what it is!

> The mission of Westfield Friends Meeting is to nurture spiritual growth and leadership in its members for the purpose of serving the community in the name of Christ.

This statement suggests an emphasis on teaching, equipping, and encouraging members. It creates an internal concentration of effort that results in a significant contribution to the external community.

As members begin to elaborate on what this statement means, some diversity of interpretation naturally emerges, but with an impressive continuity. For some, this statement means simply that the meeting will be a community based on the teachings of Jesus, with a hope that all the world might hear and accept the Good News for their lives. For others, the expanded vision uses language of "creating a safe place" where all persons are accepted and loved as they together build a witness for Jesus to the community. Friends here agree that membership at Westfield involves a commitment to this mission as a means of being faithful to Jesus Christ.

Within the structure of this meeting and mission, Westfield Friends seeks a leadership and business procedural style that empowers leaders to fulfill their charge without depriving the entire meeting of its role in decision-making. Members of the pastoral team are respected and play a key roles in decisions about mission, vision, organization, and spiritual care of the meeting. Committees also play key roles in administering programs and projects for the meeting. However, major decisions ultimately come before monthly meeting, where all participate in a process that seeks to arrive at a "sense of the meeting."

One example of the process relates to the launch of Sunday Night with Friends, which offered an alternative, contemporary style of worship designed to attract unchurched individuals from the community. Many persons in the meeting felt a leading to reach out to the community in this manner, particularly as the area was experiencing rapid growth of population. Ministry and Counsel labored for many months with the proposition and the uncertainties it raised. When committee members were of one mind, they introduced the idea at monthly meeting. After questions were answered and objections were resolved, the monthly meeting approved the new venture. Ministry and Counsel then took the initiative to prepare the members for the changes this new ministry would introduce to the meeting.

Lessons on Vitality

The landscape of America is undergoing tremendous change. Formerly rural communities are becoming the home to new populations. Cornfields are being converted into housing additions. The general store or local supermarket disappears overnight, replaced by a strip mall or other larger, commercial enterprise. Quiet county roads are becoming crowded with SUV's and minivans. The shift can feel chaotic and intimidating.

Many Friends meetings sit in the midst of just such rapid change. The meeting founded by someone's great-grandparents must decide how to react in the face of this new reality. Is it opportunity or peril? Is it a new beginning or the beginning of the end? Some of these new families entering the community will want a place to worship. If they all go elsewhere, the Friends meeting can remain a small, family chapel, but it will look like a relic of days gone by to the newly organized community. If these newcomers choose to attend the Friends meeting, the days of the small family chapel have to end, lest a two-tiered society of insiders and outsiders result.

Westfield Meeting provides some useful suggestions about how to face this change creatively. The meeting's clear identity of themselves as a Christ-centered, Quaker church provides the personal security to engage with others. Only to the degree a meeting understands itself can it disclose its identity to others. Such self-knowledge can bring confidence and security that allow it to welcome strangers. A willingness to engage the larger community is an essential predisposition. Meetings or churches who opt for a separatist mentality will, in effect, send a message of rejection to the community. This self-knowledge and willingness to engage is reflected in the Westfield Meeting's mission statement.

A second key to vitality demonstrated at Westfield is a willingness to experiment with innovative forms of worship and outreach. Such experiments will stretch a church or meeting's comfort zone, and will likely produce anxiety among those who like to avoid change. Tradition certainly has its place in the life of a faith community, but there is no escaping the fact that God sometimes calls a group to undertake new initiatives.

Westfield's Sunday Night with Friends worship service, while not unique in the larger realm of the church growth movement, is indicative of a mentality that recognizes that the Spirit may call a congregation to new things as it nurtures its members, inspires its youth, and reaches out to the unchurched. When done through careful prayer and planning, such experimentation can come without sacrifice of a group's core values or commitments. Just as it is important to be willing to try new ministries, it is equally important to be able to end experiments when they do not meet expectations and goals. Not every good idea will prove to be worth retaining—but some will.

Westfield Meeting provides a healthy reminder that human beings are social animals. Persons may possess different social needs and have different social expectations, but very few are designed for a life of isolation or hermitage. Given that reality, it should not be a surprise to find that meetings and churches can provide exceptional opportunities for nurturing satisfying friendships within the context of teaching faith and equipping for ministry. Indeed, as extended families are often separated by many miles and states, and as nuclear families are often strained and torn, finding quality friendships that are mutually beneficial can be among life's greatest challenges. Such friendships seldom develop in a larger, corporate meeting for worship for one simple reason: corporate worship is not designed to promote conversation and sharing with a small number of potential friends. For this reason, small groups play a pivotal role in the life of a meeting. These small groups may be fellowship or study groups, as is the case with Westfield. In some meetings, committees tend to provide these kinds of opportunities. In whatever small group format, to the degree this level of intimacy occurs among members, vitality will result.

Westfield Monthly Meeting
Founded: 1835
Affiliation(s): Western Yearly Meeting
                   Friends United Meeting

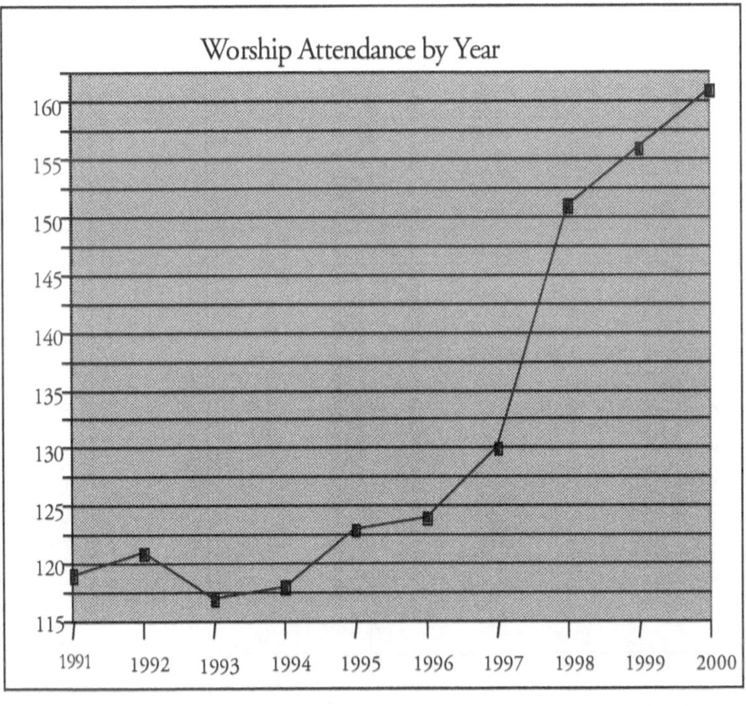

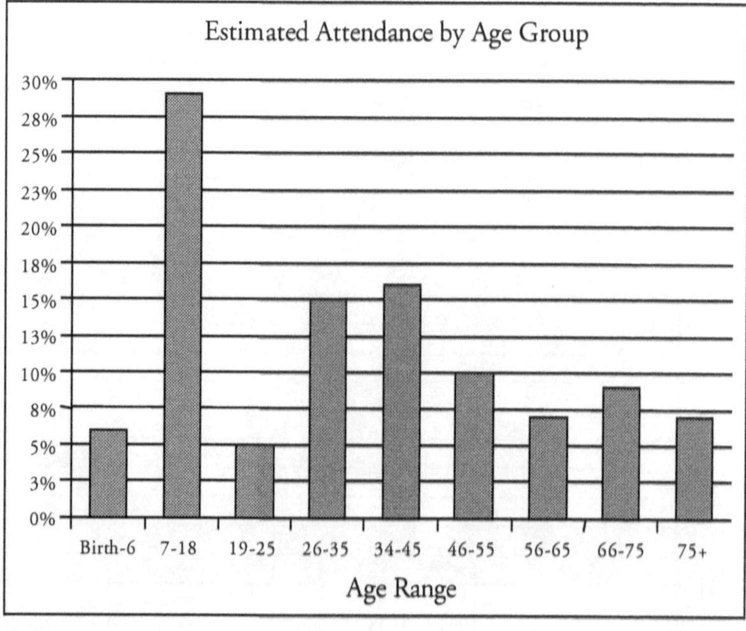
Estimated Attendance by Age Group
30%
28%
25%
23%
20%
18%
15%
13%
10%
8%
5%
3%
0%
Birth-6
7-18
19-25
26-35
34-45
46-55
56-65
66-75
75+
Age Range

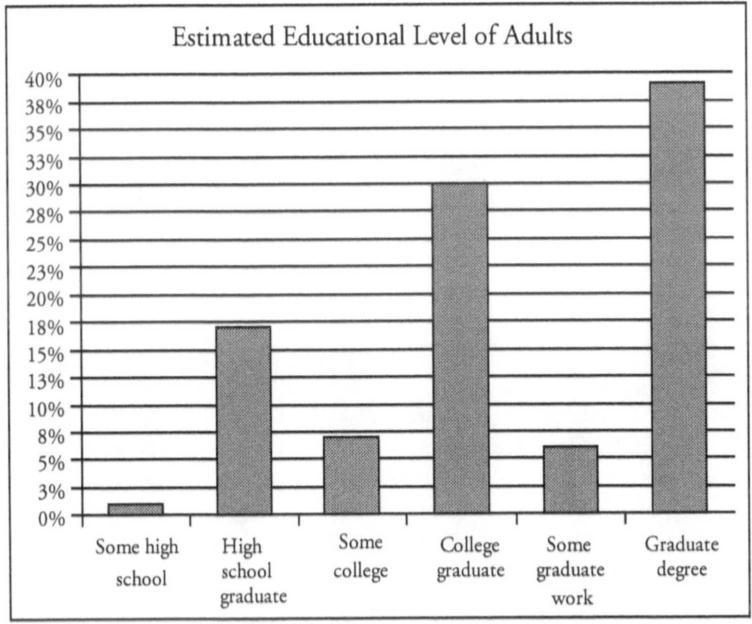
Estimated Educational Level of Adults
40%
38%
35%
33%
30%
28%
25%
23%
20%
18%
15%
13%
10%
8%
5%
3%
0%
Some high school
High school graduate
Some college
College graduate
Some graduate work
Graduate degree

Concluding Observations

This study began with a goal of surveying selected vital meetings across the Religious Society of Friends. A three-fold hope motivated this project. The primary hope was to describe and share the vital life of the participating meetings and churches. So much of what is shared among Friends emphasizes the negative aspects of our corporate life, resulting in an ethos of fear rather than trust in God and joy in the mission that has been entrusted to us. The decentralized structure of Friends makes it easy for good news to remain isolated. By collecting a few of these vital stories within one volume, this project offers a reason to hope that the future of Friends is not necessarily one of doom and dismay.

A second hope was to provide a resource for meetings and churches that are not as vital as they wish to be. This resource does not offer a "color by numbers" approach to building a vital faith community. Rather, it offers a peek into the life of the participating meetings and churches as they have reflected on their life together. This reflection gives rise to an assessment of *how* they worship, *why* they choose to worship as they do, and *where* they encounter God most meaningfully in the process. The specificity of their answers may well spark creativity in others congregations as they consider these stories and seek to discern whether any new possibilities for worship and ministry become apparent in the process. These closing pages seek to move beyond those case specific observations and offer a few comments on vitality based on the common ground observed in these nine very different locations.

Finally, it is hoped that this project might persuade other meetings to engage in a similar process of investigation and reflection. To that end, the survey instrument utilized in this study is included in the appendix. The process can be time consuming, but it can also be revealing and inspiring.

The Centrality of Worship

Based on the information collected in this study, it is reasonable to identify the act of worship as the most vitalizing component of a faith community's life together. In some ways, this sounds like an elementary comment, yet established meetings and churches can easily overlook the power of this observation. Vital worship is not equivalent to "going to meeting" or "going to church" on Sundays. It is not guaranteed by mere attendance at a service of worship. At least three useful, if not essential, characteristics can be identified.

An important characteristic of vitality is members' comfort with the style of worship practiced at the meeting or church. Worship format matters much less than the comfort of the worshipper. In the jargon of Friends, a person needs a worship format that "speaks to his or her condition." A person who needs lengthy periods of silence and little structure will not fare well with an order of service driven by a bulletin, multiple hymns, prayers and a sermon. Likewise, an individual for whom Jesus is the central figure in the salvation story will sense little spiritual edification in worship where universalistic or theistic language are the primary vehicles used to articulate the Spirit's leading. Comfort matters! Meetings and churches better serve their members and their own vitality when everyone involved understands the accepted parameters of faith and worship at that particular location. All congregations, even diverse ones, have boundaries where tolerance and comfort end and irritation begins. The better identified the boundaries are, the less chance members will cross them unintentionally or that visitors will join the meeting with unrealistic expectations.

Another important characteristic of worship is a sense of reverence for the place where worship occurs. This statement is not meant to challenge Friends' belief that people are more important than buildings. Neither is it meant to imply that the building is, in some sense, "God's house." This statement has in mind a reverence of space, not of place, merited by the quality of experience that occurs in that space when members gather for worship. Past, present, and future are united in the setting where worship occurs. Previous generations worked and worshiped together, laboring to discern God's leading for them as individuals and as a group. Echoes of past voices remain, as though spiritual residue from those experiences lingers, seasoning the present moment. Aware of that past strength, current generations sense their connectedness with a larger cloud of witnesses. Contemporary worship speaks to the need of the ones worshiping; however, it also continues the tradition and contributes to the legacy of those who will sojourn in this space in years to come. Though many meetings have no clear vision toward which the meeting aspires, there is almost always an expectation that Friends will continue to thrive and worship in these places. In that sense, there is a mental vision of a future that will be even if there is no well conceived plan of how it will be reached.

This leads to a third observation about worship in vital meetings: persons arrive for worship with a sense of expectation. What do they expect? A variety of things perhaps, but two seem especially pertinent. They expect to find a comfortable place of worship—a style and format they enjoy. They expect to experience spiritual communion as they join fellow seekers—some of whom are their closest spiritual comrades—in a sacred space where a rich, corporate communion with God is a regular occurrence. Make no mistake—Friends across the spectrum describe the communion with God differently. Some come expecting miracles in their midst. Some come to worship at the foot of their Savior's cross. Some come to meet God in the silence, and to draw communion from the deep, inner springs of the Spirit. Beneath the different language, beyond the different theology, and behind the different worship format, there is a common expectation of meeting the Living God. Vital meetings are places where these expectations are not disappointed. Worship in this manner is a far cry from a dull habit or boring routine.

Agreed-Upon Mission and Purpose

Many organizations proudly point to a concise two or three-sentence statement that summarizes their mission. Such statements make nice sidebars in printed matter or adorn office walls in attractive frames. In some cases, nearly every employee can rattle off the statement at a snap of the finger. In many instances though, these officially "adopted" statements are not widely known and have very little effect in the life of the organization. Though there is nothing wrong with such mission statements in principle, those concise statements *are not* what is referred to in this section by the words "mission" and "purpose."

As used here, statements of mission and purpose are not necessarily the product of consultants and focus groups. Instead, it is a common understanding worked out by members of the congregation that describes why this group is as it is. Whether or not it can be articulated in a precise way or reduced to a three-sentence boiler-plate statement is not important. What matters is that this common understanding is the work of the whole group, not an elite sub-group. It must be a product that has arisen from the process of their common commitment and experience together.

In the meetings and churches represented in this project, the missions certainly varied from group to group. One exists to evangelize for the sake of Jesus Christ and invite persons into accountability within a spiritual community. Another provides a place where seekers can come together without judgment to learn and grow together. Yet another creates a counter-culture within a larger, brutal, dehumanizing system. One fulfills its purpose only to the degree that Christ is glorified. Another finds that explicit Christian language creates uneasiness in the group. While each meeting or church has a spiritual focus at the core of their life together, the explicit mission and purpose of the congregations varies. In addition to the broad spiritual focus, the common thread these groups share is that various members within each group gave a similar account of what their mission is and how they were faithful to it. Able to articulate what that purpose is, vital meetings are able to self-disclose clearly to members and seekers—"this is who we are." "We exist for the purpose of A, not C. This is not to say that C is a poor choice. It is simply not our choice." Such clarity contributes to a healthy environment.

Mission and purpose do not come easily to noncreedal groups, as groups must discover what they have in common before either can be articulated. This process becomes an even greater challenge given Friends decentralized governmental structure, their understanding of business that encourages each person to voice his or her opinion, and their commitment to reach united decisions without the aid of a vote. However great of a challenge it is, a common understanding of a meeting's or church's mission and purpose is a strong contributor to vitality. It clarifies the group's identity and helps its members and attenders understand which expectations are realistic and which ones are not.

How a group answers the question of mission and purpose will have a direct impact on such things as language and songs in worship. It will influence the type of projects the meeting can embrace as corporate activities. The more homogenous a group is, the easier it will be to unite around particular projects. Supporting dissenting opinions will create a bit of corporate anxiety. A meeting with a strong commitment to evangelizing and converting sinners will be able to support activities that promote the Gospel among some population considered to be lost. They will likely have a more difficult time participating in a Christian-Muslim-

Buddhist dialogue for the purpose of understanding and accepting those faiths as valid paths to God.

Conversely, the more diverse a group is, the more difficult it can be to discover a common denominator. This contributes to the fact that in some meetings, the most a group can agree to in terms of theology is that "there is that of God in all people." This has an enormous impact on their decision to be inclusive of almost any other fellow seeker. However, discussions about the nature of God, God's interaction with the world, the nature of Jesus, or the nature of humanity seldom lead to unity. Agreeing to disagree may keep peace among the members, but it can still lead to paralysis on particular issues and projects. A convenient example is the subject of outreach. Is it evangelism or is it outreach? Is a group trying to convert or to serve? Should it be an aggressive form that seeks to persuade others to accept Jesus or should it model acceptance and tolerance of different faiths?

This project suggests that vitality can thrive in either setting among Friends. What matters most is that the meeting or church is able to agree upon its mission and purpose. From that point it is merely a matter of discovering how it will put them into practice.

London Grove and Brooklyn Meetings provide a good example of how a diverse meeting avoids paralysis in the area of mission and purpose. These are groups whose diversity limits the range and number of corporate outreach projects that can be supported by the entire meeting. While not committing the meeting as a whole to any ministry around which the entire meeting cannot unite, they do facilitate the discernment of members' calls to service and support them in a variety of ways. In this way, they are responsive to the spiritual needs of their members while remaining respectful of the many perspectives present in the meeting.

Relational Connectedness

Those who worship at vital meetings possess a sense of "belonging." It is generally not the case that members and attenders know everyone who attends the church or meeting. Even if they recognize faces and can recall names, deep relationships with all one hundred and fifty, or even sixty, members is highly unlikely. Neither will a person be able to engage with every person present on a given Sunday morning. However, it is quite possible that they have the perception of "seeing" and "interacting" with every person.

As an example, when a particular Friends meeting (not one participating in this project) rearranged the order of its two worship services and Sunday School, the time of a fifteen minute coffee social was moved as well. Attendance at the coffee social declined. Soon, some members voiced a concern that fellowship in the meeting was suffering because they no longer saw "everyone" at the coffee social. Though the meeting averaged one hundred and fifty persons in worship, approximately fifty regularly gathered for coffee. *Two thirds* of the meeting was always absent from the coffee social, so it could not be a place where those who attended saw "everyone." It was, however, a place where many relational needs were met, and in particular, a place where a certain sub-group of the meeting socialized. The absence of that intimate gathering created a relational strain in the meeting. One lesson to be learned from this experience is that however wide a person's circle of interaction is, it must be large enough that they feel deeply integrated into the life of the meeting or church. Where a sense of "belonging" occurs, vitality is nurtured.

A sense of "belonging" may be bolstered simply by having a particular bench or pew that one occupies during worship. Consciously or not, that regular seat conveys the message that this meeting has room for the individual. The church is not complete when they not present.

"Belonging" is certainly nurtured by a meaningful experience of worship that is shared with others in the room. Intimacy with God in worship creates a sense of connectedness with those who were also present when this communion occurred. It creates a common ground even if no words have been exchanged.

However, a Sunday morning corporate worship experience has its limitations in terms of building connections and deepening relationships among the group. These worship occasions limit communication between persons. It silences. It encourages listening. It invites limited vocal participation in word or in music. But it cannot create a setting where *everyone* shares their personal journey equally. Smaller groups can provide these opportunities, and among vital meetings, usually do so.

The purpose of the small group can vary. In some meetings, these are groups of persons with a common interest—parents or senior citizens. It other locations, committees serve this social and spiritual function in addition to the stated purpose of the committee.

Sometimes, clerks find themselves facilitating pastoral care in addition to the business agenda!

The activities of First Friends Indianapolis illustrate a three-fold function of these groups: spiritual formation, fellowship, and outreach. These groups provide a forum for more direct communication among individuals than can occur in meeting for worship on Sunday mornings. Whatever the foci of the groups, in vital meetings, they frequently provide a deeper anchor into the network of relationships within the meeting. They allow a person to know and be better known among a few persons, providing nurture, care and a sense of belonging.

Service Opportunities

Friends choose to be Friends for a variety of reasons. Some are continuing a family heritage. Others are refugees from an overzealous version of Christianity that inflicted wounds instead of healing them. Some are attracted by the contemplative lifestyle, the noncreedal faith, or the social testimonies. Some found salvation through the evangelistic efforts of Quakers in their community. Whatever the attraction, members of vital meetings sing a common song that faith as practiced by Friends has something to contribute to the larger society. This suggests that at some point the question of service opportunities is an appropriate one for meetings and churches to consider. The term "service" is being used here as an alternative to evangelism or outreach, each of which carries its own complicated connotations.

Vital meetings always find ways to contribute to the larger community where they are located. The participants in this project display a wide range of involvement. Riverside Friends Church undertakes evangelistic ministries which involve several members of the congregation. It is approved and supported by the church. It draws wide participation from the group. The church's identity is largely shaped by this commitment to service in the form of evangelism. Likewise, Brooklyn Meeting's decision to offer escorts to Muslim and Arabic persons in the area was a project embraced by the meeting and which publicly displayed the meeting's commitment to diversity and peace based on spiritual values. The Sing Sing Worship Group participates in an ambitious project of transforming a cultural ethos with its involvement in Alternative to Violence workshops. As an example of a different type of service, some of Newtown Meeting's and West Richmond Meeting's most significant service to the community occurs in the form of leadership offered to boards of Quaker and community organizations. This form of service is carried forth by members, not an entire meeting; but the motivation for service rises from the spiritual practice experienced in the life of the meeting.

Whatever form it may take, this activity of service is mutually beneficial. For the persons offering service, it allows them to be faithful to the Holy Spirit's nudge towards ministry, as well as to experience the satisfaction of having helped others. For those receiving the ministry, acts of service meet particular needs they have and invite them to consider issues related to God and faith. For the meeting or church, service activities contribute to vitality in at least two ways. As service opportunities deepen the spiritual journey of members, meetings and churches benefit from that increased depth. These opportunities also contribute to the breadth of a meeting's engagement with the larger community, and shape the community's understanding of them.

Vision for the Future

If the meetings and churches involved in this study are an accurate indication, Friends are not prone to have formal visioning processes and strategic plans. This is not to say that it never occurs, but it is not the norm. Formal planning often occurs only when a specific need or crisis motivates action. Despite the missing formality, vital meetings appear to possess two important characteristics related to a vision for the future.

First, even without a specific plan, these meetings and churches have a strong optimism about the future. The fear of aging populations and declining numbers that is prominent in many places does not burden these Friends. In the midst of a setting that feeds their own spiritual hunger, these Friends feel confident that the vigor of the meeting will continue indefinitely. They know they have a purpose beyond the ritual of gathering. Whether they describe it in terms of seeking, nurturing or witnessing, they understand that they are engaged in important work. And whether they use language such as "working for the kingdom of God" or "seeking truth wherever it may be found" the value of this work outweighs any concern about timelines or numbers. This optimism, which is dually fed by their own experience and the larger sense of purpose, wields a certain degree of power.

Second, these vital meetings succeed without formal processes because they have a commitment to dialogue and process. This commitment invites members to participate in the planning process. In a manner appropriate to Friends, these plans are not dictated by the upper echelons of a hierarchy. They emerge after the Friends consider matters, whether in retreat settings or in meeting for worship for business.

Whether an annual planning session or the periodic engagement of consultants followed by sustained conversation about the consultant's report, vital meetings and churches devote some time to introspection and reflection. Westfield's experiment with a contemporary service came from this type of careful conversation at several locations within the meeting. Atlanta's decision to locate the meetinghouse in a particular part of the city represents the same kind of careful conversation. So does West Richmond's move to a team ministry approach. In instances such as these, time is allowed to ask what are the new things to which God calls them? This allows for the possibility that a portion of ministry remains fresh and responsive to the present moment, even as some routine activities will always need the group's attention.

Creating a vital meeting is not accomplished by following a simple formula. The Spirit of God blows wherever it wishes. Without that fresh wind, dead bones remain dead bones. Recognizing the priority of that foundational reality, the five general traits identified in these concluding observations can be named as characteristics of meetings and churches that demonstrate genuine vitality, and are suggested as worthy of consideration by meetings who aspire to greater vitality than they currently enjoy.

Appendix
Earlham School of Religion
Monthly Meeting Vitality Study

Name of Meeting:

Yearly Meeting Affiliation:

Name of Person(s) Completing Form:

Ministry

1. How does the meeting or church understand the concept of ministry? For instance, is ministry valued? Is it important? Is it the responsibility of one person, a few, or everyone?

2. If ministry is valued, how is it modeled in the meeting? For instance, is ministry among the group authoritative, consultative, egalitarian? What role does the leading of the Spirit play in ministry?

3. Does the meeting help its members and attenders discern their spiritual gifts and calls to ministries? If so, how is this done?

4. How does the meeting nurture those persons who sense gifts for or calls to ministry in terms of education, oversight, and/or practice.

5. What ministries does the meeting or church provide to its members and attenders? How did those begin?

What percentage of the meeting or church participates in these ministries?

6. What ministries or outreach does the meeting or church provide to the immediate community? How many people participate in these ministries?

7. Do the ministries described in questions 5 and 6 attract new attenders to the meeting or church?

Theology

8. Communities require some commonalities. In religious communities, these are sometimes based on common beliefs or values, common practices, or both. Is your meeting or church more aligned based on beliefs and values, practices, or both?

9. What beliefs or values are central to the meeting's or church's faith?

10. How are these central beliefs and values reflected in the lives of members and attenders?

11.What role do particularly Quaker testimonies or interpretations of commonly held beliefs play in the meeting's or church's organization and ministry?

12. How are these Quaker testimonies and interpretations reflected in the lives of members and attenders?

13. How does personal experience factor into the shaping of belief and practice?

14. What is the relationship between faith and practice?

15. What is the relationship between worship and practice?

Visioning and Business Processes
16. Does the meeting or church have a vision for its future? If so, summarize it in a paragraph.

17. How was this vision, or how are other major decisions, determined?

18. How does this vision relate to the manner of worship and the types of activities at the meeting or church?

19. Is leadership recognized as such in your meeting or church? If so, what style of leadership is valued? For instance, is leadership permanent within a position, or temporary by task or committee assignment? Is leadership authoritative, consultative, or egalitarian?

20. Does the meeting or church reach decisions by "sense of the meeting" or by another process?

21. If your meeting or church has pastoral leadership, what role does the pastor play in these processes?

Community Life
22. How often are meeting or church members and attenders together other than on Sunday? What types of

occasions bring them together? What percentage of the meeting or church participates in these occasions?

23. Of the types of community activities listed below, please rank their level of importance as determined by participation:

> Worship   ______
> Small Groups ______
> Bible Study   ______
> Work Projects______
> Other   ______

24. Which is the more important role of the meeting or church: creating a place for relationships to form, or communicating God's truth?

25. What areas of activity in the life of the meeting or church generate the greatest amount of enthusiasm and energy?

26. What areas of activity drain the greatest amount of energy from the meeting or church?

27. Has the community around the meeting or church changed significantly in recent years? For instance, has the area become more populated or less populated? Has the community become more diverse racially, ethnically, economically, or in other ways?

28. If the community has changed, how has the meeting or church adjusted to these changes? Were these changes perceived as a threat or an opportunity? What percentage

of the current members and attenders live within the community? How engaged is the meeting or church with the immediate community?